TABLE OF CONTENTS

ACRONYMS

CJCS	Chairman Joint Chiefs of Staff
DIME	Diplomacy, Information, Military, and Economics
DOD	Department of Defense
DOS	Department of State
DOTMLPF	Doctrine, Organization, Training, Materiel, Leadership, Personnel, and Facilities
LTG	Lieutenant General
GEN	General
IMF	International Monetary Fund
MG	Major General
MNLA	Movement for the Liberation of Azawad
NATO	North Atlantic Treaty Organization
NMS	National Military Strategy
NSS	United States National Security Strategy
OPEC	Organization of Petroleum Exporting Countries
ORHA	Office for Reconstruction and Humanitarian Assistance
PCI	Per Capita Income
PMESII	Political, Military, Economic, Social, Infrastructure, and Information
SECDEF	Secretary of Defense
TRADOC	Training and Doctrine Command
TRISA	U.S. Army TRADOC Intelligence Support Activity
UN	United Nations
USAID	United States Agency for International Development

ILLUSTRATIONS

AMERICA'S TRANSITIONAL BACKGROUND:
FROM REVOLUTION TO IRAQ

After over 200 years of shifting from war to peace, America's turbulent transitions in Iraq and Afghanistan demonstrate the need for a more adaptable military construct capable of building interconnected globalized systems that create stability. America's history reveals its tendencies towards applying force as a way to achieve its strategic objectives. During the 1940s, the United States transitioned from war to stabilizing peace with Germany and Japan while simultaneously creating democracies, globalized economics, and international institutions to achieve mutual security. However, America's history of war, expansion, and stabilization goes further back than its more recent role as a world leader.

The United States is a nation-state forged from war. A successful revolution separated America from the colonial British Empire. Even before the United States declared independence on 4 July 1776, American had already begun the process of transitioning from war to the task of building a democratic government with unique values and aspirations. Shortly after independence, the original Thirteen Colonies pushed to expand American hegemony westward. Each period of expansion involved transitioning from conflict to stability, and then finally to civilian control. The growth was not without its share of hardships, conflict, and sometimes shameful actions by all parties involved.

During the Westward Expansion between 1776 and 1890, America sought not to colonize the lands held by Native Americans, but to subsume the land into its ever-expanding empire.[1] Early American policy reinforced the actions of expansionists as they pushed toward the Pacific Ocean. A policy advocated by the Secretary of War, John C. Calhoun in 1817 to move "Indians"

---

[1]George C. Herring, *From Colony to Superpower: U.S. Foreign Relations since 1776* (New York: Oxford University Press, 2008), 41-60, 145-8, 172-174.

beyond the 95th meridian became law in 1825.[2] Hard power was often the way to enforce this policy. Once in control of an area, the pioneers had to first establish security, create independent districts with local governance, institute rule of law, and build infrastructure to support economic growth before it sought acceptance into the Union.[3] These tasks often overlapped one another and were not completed sequentially. The main point is that there was a period of conflict followed by a period of stability. By 1912, the nation-building efforts of the pioneers created a united nation of 48 states. However, even before the unification was complete, America enacted policies to spread its ideas and values to other nations around the world.[4] Expanding the ideas of the American way of life is what Walter McDougall called the "new testament" of American foreign policy.[5]

The Spanish-American War in 1898 opened the door to American nation-building efforts abroad. The United States' annexation of the Philippines from the Spanish is arguably the first instance where American grand strategy went through multiple transitional periods between 1898 and 1934. First, this new strategy used war for the purpose of regime change. The strategy then transitioned to fighting another war against Filipino insurgents while simultaneously conducting

---

[2]Andrew J. Bacevich, *American Empire: The Realities and Consequences of U.S. Diplomacy* (Cambridge, MA/London, 2002), 203.

[3]The Confederation Congress adopted on 13 July 1787, the Northwest Ordinance, officially titled "An Ordinance for the Government of the Territory of the United States North West of the River Ohio," prescribed six articles required of a district before it could become a state. Confederation Congress, "An Ordinance for the Government of the Territory of the United States North West of the River Ohio," Library of Congress, http://www.loc.gov/rr/program/bib/ourdocs/northwest.html (accessed 8 December 2012).

[4]Herring, 301-9.

[5]Walter McDougall, *The Constitutional History of U.S. Foreign Policy: 222 Years of Tension in the Twilight Zone* (Philadelphia, PA: Foreign Policy Research Institute, September 2010) http://www.fpri.org/pubs/2010/McDougall.ConstitutionalHistoryUSForeignPolicy.pdf (accessed 10 November 2012), 5.

nation-building operations. Lastly, the strategy transitioned turning over operations to host nation

civil control.[6] The strategic approach taken in the Philippines between 1898 and 1934 remains in

military doctrine today: seize initiative (Phase II); dominate the enemy force (Phase III); stabilize

the country (Phase IV); and finally enable civil authority (Phase V).[7] The important aspect of this

approach is actions during previous phases affect the actions during later phases. The system

continues to evolve in order to achieve its purpose. President William McKinley's desire to keep

his options open during Phase II led to the deployment of military ground forces and the

occupation of the Philippines for the next thirty years.[8]

Research Question and Scope

Since the Spanish-American War, politicians have used military force as a way of

promoting American ideas numerous times. This hard power use of military capabilities remains

unchanged today. The 2010 United States National Security Strategy (NSS) continues to promote

the expansion of the same ideas held in 1898 of peace, freedom, and free markets abroad.[9] The

question is whether war or military intervention is the correct form of national diplomacy to

accomplish these strategic aims remains up for debate.

This monograph does not claim that all future American conflicts aim to promote these

same ideas, nor does it imply that America should use the military as its primary means of

---

[6]Brian McAllister Linn, *The U.S. Army and Counterinsurgency in the Philippine War, 1899-1902.* (Chapel Hill: University of North Carolina Press, 1989), 2. Also see Herring, 309-36, 365-67, 634.

[7]U.S. Department Of Defense. *Joint Operations.* Joint Publication 3-0. (Washington DC: 11 August 2011), V-6. The other two phases are Phase 0 is shaping operations, and Phase I is deter.

[8]Herring, 20. Herring suggests that missionary and business expansionists help persuade President McKinley to occupy the Philippines.

[9]Office of the President, *The National Security Strategy of the United States of America* (Washington, DC: The White House, May 2010), i-ii.

diplomacy. There are a vast number of alternative methods for making American ideas and way of life more attractive to foreign governments. America's diplomatic, economic, and information efforts must be incorporated into all planning efforts during every phase of a military operation or engagement. Subsequent phases have causal links to all actions from previous phases. The idea is that Phase III and Phase IV are inseparable during planning and required a collective interagency plan to facilitate a successful transition. The second idea is that Phase IV consists of rebuilding host nation capacity and control in an interconnected globalized manner. The scope of this paper is limited by these two philosophies when war, otherwise known as Clausewitzian diplomacy, is applied.

The first philosophy is if America destroys another nation, it is America's responsibility to rebuild it either unilaterally or through a multinational coalition. Colin Powell's arguments when he tried to deter the invasion into Iraq encompassed this philosophy: "Once you break it, you are going to own it, and we're going to be responsible for 26 million people standing there looking at us."[10] This philosophy requires the military to execute Phase III and then transition to Phase IV.

The second philosophy, one shared by Thomas Friedman and Thomas Barnett, is that reconstruction efforts overhaul the country in a globalized manner. The argument is that economic globalization promotes interconnectedness that facilitates lasting peace.[11] This philosophy requires a military capable of winning the war during Phase III in such a way that allows for a rapid transition to Phase IV. Again, the term *transition* incorporates two different

---

[10]Colin Powell, "Ideas and Consequences" (Lecture, Aspen Ideas Festival, Aspen, Colorado, July 2007), http://www.theatlantic.com/magazine/archive/2007/10/ideas-and-consequences/306193/ (accessed 9 December 2012).

[11]Thomas P.M. Barnett, *The Pentagon's New Map: War and Peace in the Twenty-First Century* (New York: Berkley Trade, 2005); Thomas L. Friedman, *The Lexus and the Olive Tree* (New York: Farrar, Straus and Giroux, 2000).

concepts. First, the United States will go to war and transition from Phase III to Phase IV. Second, actions conducted by the United States prior to and during Phase III affect the transition process and required actions during Phase IV. Therefore, the research in this monograph focuses on the important and under-studied aspect of transitions in warfare.

Chapter 2 covers four different aspects that surround the complexity of war. The first section provides a definition for strategy and the various levels of strategy. America's national policy, grand strategy, and laws shape the military during peacetime and war. They play a role in shaping the doctrine, organization, training, materiel, leadership, personnel, and facilities (DOTMLPF) of the military. The DOTMLPF framework determines the capabilities of the military, the employment of the military, and the military's capacity to transition between phases.[12] The second section of the literature review describes how the United States sees its role in the world and why. This helps to understand why America goes to war and the goals it has for peace afterwards. Section three of the literature review provides a definition for systems and covers the system theories of Robert Jervis, Peter Senge, and Jahmsid Gharjidehgi[13]. System theory provides the concept behind why military actions in Phase III affect the transition and rebuilding requirements in Phase IV. The fourth section outlines the concept of post-Cold War globalization and its impact on stability. The two leading commentators on globalization and geopolitics included in this paper are Thomas Friedman and Thomas Barnett. Friedman's theory discusses the interconnected systems as required for economic growth, but balances it against national culture, traditions, and geography. Although, he admits that globalization will not end

---

[12]Joint Publication 3-0, 14-5.

[13]Robert Jervis, *System Effects* (Princeton, New Jersey: Princeton University Press, 1998); Peter M. Senge, *The Fifth Discipline: the Art and Practice of the Learning Organization*, Rev. and updated. ed. (New York: Crown Business, 2006); Jamshid Gharajedaghi, *Systems Thinking: Managing Chaos and Complexity: a Platform for Designing Business Architecture*, 2nd ed. (Boston, MA: Butterworth-Heinemann, 2006).

geopolitics.[14] Barnett further expands on this theory and applies it to potential areas of future conflict around the globe.

Chapter 3 provides historical examples of the military's strategy during war and the stability operations that followed. Using Alexander George's case study methodology, the two cases used in this monograph are World War II and the 2003 Iraq War.[15] The four different areas outlined in the literature review are used to analyze each historical example. The case studies seek to answer the following questions. Why did the United States go to war, and what were the desired outcomes? What were the ways and means the United States used, deliberately or inadvertently, to destroy the enemy's political, military, economic, social, infrastructure, and information (PMESII) systems prior to transitioning to Phase IV? How did the transition from Phases III to Phase IV happen? What means did the United States possess prior to transition to facilitate achieving the ends? Did the United States intend to rebuild the nation into a globalized system prior to the end of Phase III?

Chapter 4 concludes with a summary of the literature review and case studies. The second section describes the military's ability to quickly transition from the dominate phase of operations into stability. It describes the Stability Phase and its focus to rebuild a country destroyed by war. The next section describes the military's inability to make rapid progress at the start of Phase IV. It provides additional research questions and additional considerations. The closing outlines why the United States military must adapt its DOTMLPF framework to facilitate nation-building operations.

---

[14]Friedman, 250.

[15]Alexander L. George and Andrew Bennett, *Case Studies and Theory Development in the Social Sciences* (Cambridge, MA: The MIT Press, 2005), 61-73.

Methodology

The purpose of this monograph is to examine the United States' approach to war through the transition and follow-on stability operations as it seeks to create lasting stability around the world. The focus is on the transition between Phase III and Phase IV. The basis for this study is how military ways and means support the National Security Strategy in an interconnected era of globalization. As the world's only superpower, the United States maintains an unprecedented role in global affairs, international connectivity, and regional stability. Globalization will continue to define America's role and position around the world.

The concept of globalization entails six interrelated systems described in Joint Publication 2-01.3 as political, military, economic, social, infrastructure, and information (PMESII).[16] These six systems align with Thomas Friedman's definition of globalization and encapsulate systems theory.[17] The United States military regularly targets these enemy systems during operations in order to destroy, shock, or modify them. The intent of targeting these systems is to change their purpose in such a way that the modified system aligns closer with American interests. Figure 1 shows how as operations move from Phase I to Phase III military force increases, systems capabilities decrease, and governmental and non-governmental agencies leave the country during the actual fighting. Appendix A provides the notional operation plan phases versus the level of military effort during each phase. One can easily discern from the diagram the level of effort on dominate activities during Phase III.

---

[16]U.S. Department Of Defense, *Joint Intelligence Preparation of the Operational Environment*. Joint Publication 2-01.3 (Washington, DC: 16 June 2009), II-44. It is worth acknowledging that there is a current debate about religious extremist organizations. The debate centers on classification of activities inside a state or if they form non-state actors. This debate is outside the scope of this paper. Religious activities fall under the social system in which the U.S. is involved.

[17]Friedman, xvii-xxii.

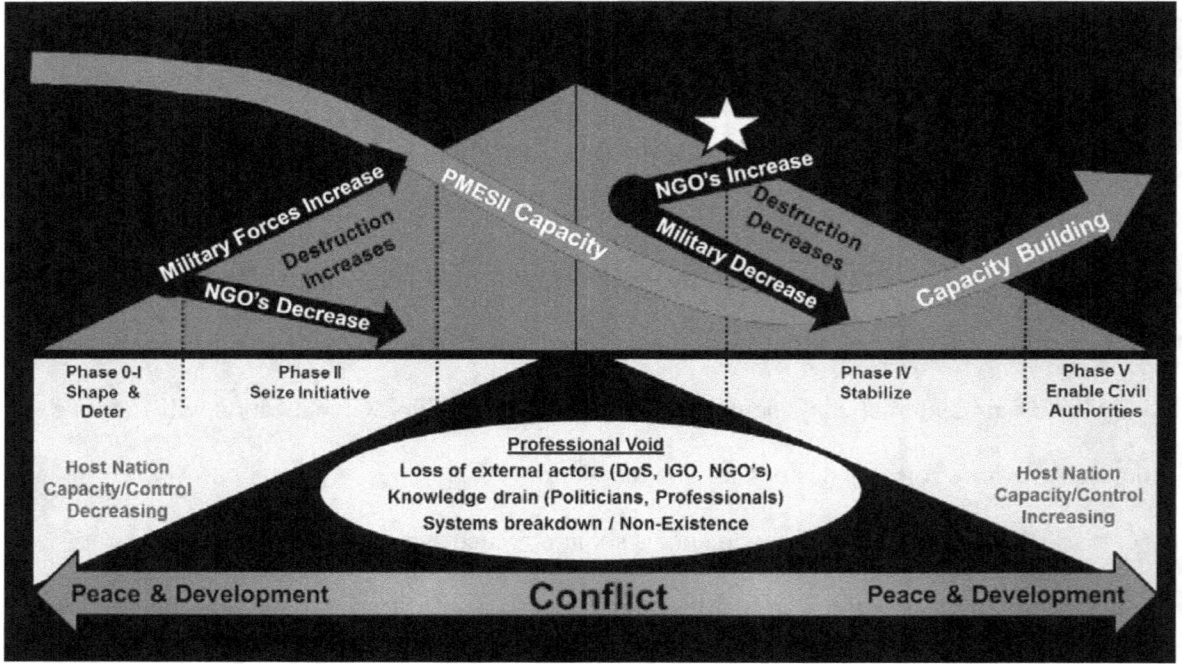

Figure 1. Systems Capacity through the Conflict Continuum.

Source: Created by the author to help graphically display interconnected relationships.

The military transitions from the dominate phase to the stability phase once it has achieved its objective. The intent of the stability phase is to build systems that facilitate the continuation of peace and economic growth. Although Joint Doctrine describes Phase IV as the stabilize phase, stability operations are present during all five phases. Appendix B shows notional balance of offensive, defensive, and stability operations during each phase. Political policy will determine when the United States moves from Phase IV into Phase V. Once military diplomacy is no longer required, a political decision is made to transition to civil control.

Military planners develop the ways that the military uses to achieve political objectives. The important point here is that planners can only develop ways to achieve political success by using the available means at the time. Secretary of Defense (SECDEF) Donald Rumsfeld put it,

"You go to war with the Army you have. They're not the Army you might want or wish to have at a later time."[18] The concept remains the same outside of war in that the military shapes, deters, seizes the initiative, dominates, conducts stability operations, and transitions to civil control with the force structure that it has. It is within the area of ways and means this monograph seeks to identify a better way towards approaching the various systems of a country before, during, and after conflict. The military must change aspects within the DOTMLPF framework to better recognize the impacts that Phases 0 through III have on the country's PMESII systems; establish a better understanding and working relationship with other governmental departments outside the military to rapidly facilitate transition between Phase III and IV; and adapt its means to increase the ways available to political decision makers to achieve their desired goals.

LITERATURE REVIEW

Strategy, Theory, and Background

The President of the United States publishes the National Security Strategy on average of every three to four years.[19] This document guides America's strategic approach for advancing its national interests. Each department within the U.S. Government refines this approach within their applicable areas, and then publishes further guidance for its department. Appendix C shows how the Department of Defense (DOD) and Department of State (DOS) translate grand strategy into future operations and force structure. Therefore, one must understand how policies are developed and how they determine the military's role in national security in order to evaluate military

---

[18]Thomas E. Ricks, *Fiasco: The American Military Adventure in Iraq, 2003 to 2005*, Reprint ed. (New York, NY: Penguin Books, 2007), 412.

[19]U.S. Department Of Defense, *Joint Operation Planning*. Joint Publication 5-0. (Washington DC: 11 August 2011), xi. JP 5-0 states, "The National Security Strategy (NSS) is a comprehensive report required annually by Title 50, USC, Section 404a. . . . Although the NSS is an annual requirement, it typically is not updated for several years at a time and may be superseded by other strategic documents and policy statements."

capabilities. The available military means constrains how the military can defeat a country during Phase III. The means also constrains its options to rebuild the country during Phase IV to meet political aims. The military's current capabilities and doctrine limits its approach as it moves through the phases of an operation from shape to dominate to stability. This limitation or gap between grand strategy and military capabilities creates the discourse towards future change in the military DOTMLPF structure.

Congressional and military staffs formulate different strategies in order to shape and control the future. The strategies later serve as an explanation for actions taken by America and the decisions made. For instance, the current strategic guidance helps to answer why stability operations are vital to American national interest, and why they continue today. Using past strategies as a guide, one can answer questions such as how does the NSS guide foreign policy and actions during wartime, and what are its reasons for stability operations? How does the National Military Strategy (NMS) shape military structure? Why does the military seek to destroy certain enemy PMESII systems in Phase III, only to rebuild them during Phase IV? Does the current NSS require military involvement to facilitate nation-building operations or is the military the only force large enough to conduct such operations? How is DOD, more specifically the Department of the Army, set up to perform these types of operations? The majority of the applicable strategies are 2010 National Security Strategy, the 2012 strategic defense guidance entitled, *Sustaining U.S. Global Leadership: Priorities for the 21st Century Defense*, 2011 National Military Strategy, and various DOD doctrinal manuals and posture statements.[20] Although many of these documents contain the word *strategy* in the title, there are several different levels of strategy within the overall framework.

---

[20]The National Security Strategy-2010; U.S. Department Of Defense, *Sustaining U.S. Global Leadership: Priorities for the 21st Century Defense.* (Washington DC: January 2012).

The literature review provides a basic understanding of U.S. strategy and of the theories used to create these strategies. This typology is necessary to analyze each case study. These theories include systems theory, complexity theory, liberal institutionalism, globalization, and economic entanglements to maintain peace, America's role in a globalized world, and why America should continue to retain the role of world leadership. Within each of these theories lies an approach to military domination during war that facilitates transition to a stable peace.

Strategy Defined: National, Military, and Operational

There are as many interpretations of the word strategy as there are different levels in which society and governments apply the term. The civil sector has strategies for business, economics, and even marketing. Within the United States government, there are national, grand, joint, military, and operational strategies. Carl von Clausewitz defines strategy as the, "the use of engagements for the purpose of war."[21] Hew Strachan makes the case that the term *strategy* only applies to military ways in his article, *The Lost Meaning of Strategy*. He states, "Strategy is designed to make war useable by the state, so that it can, if need be, use force to fulfill its political objectives. One of the reasons we are unsure what war is that we are unsure about what strategy is or is not. It is not policy; it is not politics; it is not diplomacy. It exists in relation to all three, but it does not replace them."[22] The weakness of these definitions is that they limit strategy to the use of military force or the threat of military force as it applies to fighting. What then does one call

---

[21]Carl von Clausewitz, *On War,* ed. and trans. Michael Howard and Peter Paret. (Princeton, NJ: Princeton University Press, 1976), 177. See also 75, 128, 227. Clausewitz describes war as nothing but a duel on a larger scale. He defines war as: "War is thus an act of [physical] force to compel our enemy to do our will . . . means of war; to impose our will on the enemy is its object." He later defines engagements as fighting, with the object of fighting to destroy or defeat the enemy.

[22]Thomas Mahnken and Joseph A. Maiolo, eds., *Strategic Studies: a Reader* (New York: Routledge, 2008), 421-5.

the DOS's efforts in Afghanistan over the past ten years, if not strategy since both DOS and DOD have the same overarching political aim as the military? The United States' National Security Strategy promotes the use of all elements of national power to secure a position of greater advantage: diplomacy, information, military, and economics (DIME).

In today's global society, international policies apply military means to peacekeeping operations with the purpose to prevent conflict.[23] Although this might fall under Clausewitz's idea of the threat of force, the U.S. military force capabilities applied are often too limited to achieve that mandate. Clausewitz makes it clear that a nation must continue to apply additional force against the enemy until that nation meets its strategic aim. However, if the necessary means are not available, then the nation must negotiate terms.[24]

In an attempt to achieve these desired aims, the U.S. military has expanded its capabilities beyond just the fighting forces with functional areas such as Civil Affairs, Public Affairs, and Foreign Area Officers. The primary mission of these branches is to entice a potential aggressor to use ways other than violence to achieve their desired objectives. Sun Tzu describes this concept of achieving one's objectives without fighting as supreme excellence in military leadership.[25] The NSS clearly states that the U.S. aims are to promote peace, security, opportunity, freedom, democracy, and connect through international trade. How then does the military adjust its DOTMLPF structure to meet these strategic aims?

---

[23]United Nations, "United Nations Peacekeeping," United Nations, http://www.un.org/en/peacekeeping/ (accessed 7 November 2012). In 2012, the United States was involved in seven of the sixteen United Nations peacekeeping operations around the world. The mission of these peacekeeping forces maintains a similar theme: protection of human rights, implementation of the rule-of-law-structures, and strengthen governmental institutions.

[24]Clausewitz, 77-8.

[25]Sun Tzu, *The Art of War* (New York: Barnes & Noble Classics, 2003), 15. "Hence to fight and conquer in all your battles is not supreme excellence; supreme excellence consists in breaking the enemy's resistance without fighting."

First, a thorough understanding of the definitions and the level at which the word strategy or strategic aims applies is needed before one can evaluate the various strategies themselves. These different levels and documents are in part why the military seeks to destroy part of an enemy's PMESII systems during Phase III to win wars, knowing they have to rebuild them in Phase IV to achieve a lasting peace. Below is a list of theorists and their definitions for the term strategy and the level at which they apply.

Grand Strategy: Everett C. Dolman states, "A plan for attaining continuing advantage. For the goal of strategy is not to culminate events, or to establish finality in the discourse between states, but to influence states' discourse in such a way that it will go forward on favorable terms."[26] B.H. Liddell Hart describes grand strategy as, "a way to coordinate and direct all the resources of a nation, or band of nations, towards the attainment of the political object of the war – the goal defined by fundamental policy."[27] At this level, the government can apply any of the elements of national power (DIME).

Strategy: Hart defines this level as, "the art of applying military means to fulfill the ends of policy."[28] Clausewitz describes strategy as a state in being, and not a series of events. He states, "Strategy is the use of engagements for the object of war. The original means of strategy is victory – that is, tactical success; its ends, in the final analysis are those objects which lead directly to peace."[29] Colin Gray describes strategy as the bridge that relates military power to political purpose. He states, "Strategy refers to the use made of operations for their impact upon

---

[26]Everett Carl Dolman, *Pure Strategy: Power and Principle in the Space and Information Age* (New York: Frank Cass, 2005), 6.

[27]B.H. Liddell Hart, *Strategy*, 2nd ed. (New York: Praeger Publishers, Inc., 1974), 322.

[28]Hart, 321

[29]Clausewitz, 177.

the course and outcome of war."[30] At this level, the government uses the military as its primary means to achieve its political aims during war.

Military Strategy: The U.S. military doctrine describes the purpose of military strategy, "is to link military means with the political aims in pursuit of continuing advantage."[31] At this level, the military determines how it shapes its force so that it has the capacity to achieve the stated political aims. This level of strategy plays a key part in how the military determines its DOTMPLF framework.

Operational Strategy: Dolman states, "The purpose of operational strategy is to contest or gain command of the medium (land, sea, air, space, information), which allows the tactical and political aims to remain at odds logically but to converge practically."[32] Operational strategy is the practical adaptation of the means to achieve the political objective. Baron de Jomini connects operational strategy with tactics when he defines grand tactics as, "the art of posting troops upon the battle-field according to the accidents of the ground, bringing them into action and the art of fighting upon the ground, in contradistinction to the planning upon the map."[33]

Politicians often use a "whole of government" approach to achieve a political condition. This approach may or may not include military means. The holistic approach has the same meaning as grand strategy and the employment of DIME. When the level of strategy is unclear, it is difficult to identify exactly where grand strategy ends and operational strategy begins, much

---

[30]Colin S. Gray, *War, Peace and International Relations: an Introduction to Strategic History* (London: Routledge, 2007), 40.

[31]Joint Publication 3-0, 14-5.

[32]Dolman, 30.

[33]Baron de Jomini, *Summary of the Art of War*, Translated from the French by Capt. G. H. Mendell and Lieut W.P. Craighill, Westport, CT: Greenwood, 1992. First Published by J.B. Lippincott & Co, 24-25.

less where military strategy fits into the picture at all. There are three reasons to delineate the four different levels of strategy. The first reason is to distinguish how politicians seek to create an environment for sustainable peace through either a whole of government approach or the use of violence. A second reason is to distinguish between actions conducted by the military during peacetime and that of war. The third reason is to provide a term that separates the arrangements of tactical actions from that of strategy.

For the sake of clarity, the four levels of strategy apply in the following ways. America's Grand Strategy employs all elements of diplomacy, information, military and economics (DIME) for a whole of government approach to achieve the desired political objectives. Strategy entails the political use of military means to achieve a political aim. Military strategy determines the development, structure, and preparation of military forces during peacetime. Operational Strategy is the tactical application of military means, over time and space, to achieve a political aim.

American policy and strategies will continue to dictate how the military shapes and applies their capabilities around the world. Current strategies cover military operations from political alliances to unilateral operations aimed at defeating Al Qaida.[34] American military capabilities will often be only part of a whole of government approach to secure a future advantage for the United States.[35] The 2010 National Security Strategy is one of several grand strategies that reflect America's desire to maintain its position as the world leader. These foreign and domestic strategies guide military force structure and actions around the world.

---

[34]Sustaining U.S. Global Leadership, 1-6.

[35]Ibid., 1.

<u>United States' Role in the World and Its Strategic Guidance</u>

American foreign policy continues to evolve with the world around it. Different policies and strategies were necessary at certain times to protect American interest and sustain ascension.[36] Policies to promote economic growth and encourage free societies have endured throughout U.S. history. The policies and strategies of a given period determined whether the U.S. went to war or not, what its strategic aims were if it did go to war, and how long it remained to ensure regional stability. For researches purposes, this paper focuses on periods when the United States went to war and remained for nation-building operations. However, one cannot focus solely on the foreign policy of the time without knowing how American policy developed and the implications those policies had on the military. Since each of these ideologies still exist today, planners must consider them when looking to shape military operations and DOTMLPF structure.

Walter Mead describes some of these foreign policies and strategies, aligning them to prominent statesmen in American history. He outlines four basic ways that Americans approach world affairs: Jacksonian, Jeffersonian, Hamiltonian, and Wilsonian.[37] The first school of thought is Jacksonian, which focuses U.S. policy on physical security and economic strength of the American populace. The concept states that one's ability to exceed or fail on his own determines

---

[36]Office of the President, *The National Security Strategy of the United States of America* (Washington, DC: The White House, January 1987), 4; The National Security-2010, 7. There are both difference and similarities between the two National Security Strategies even though they are only 23 years apart. The security strategy in 1987 focused on the major threat of ommunism and the Soviet Union, whereas today's external threat focuses on Al-Qaeda and global terrorism. More importantly are the similarities between the two, such as the security of the U.S. and its allies, the control of nuclear weapons, and focusing on sustainment of U.S. global leadership and power. It is the later security strategy of sustaining international order by U.S. leadership that requires the military to maintain a nation-build capability within its force structure.

[37]Walter R. Mead, *Special Providence: American Foreign Policy and How It Changed the World* (New York: Taylor & Francis Books, Inc., 2002), xvi-xviii.

his choice of freedom. Jacksonians believe that America should apply extreme military force when attacked or threatened, such as the Japanese attacks on Pearl Harbor and Al-Qaeda attacks on the World Trade Center. Remarkably similar to the Powell doctrine, operations abroad should be clearly tied to a political goal, and armed forces returned home quickly.[38] Therefore, any changes to the U.S. military force structure or doctrine should consider how to accomplish the political goals as quickly as possible, leaving only a small force behind if any force at all in order to protect America's interest.

The second school of thought is that of the Jeffersonians, which seeks to protect American interest at home and argue against international agreements.[39] This concept sees attempts to spread democracy, global systems, and international alliances as poor policy.[40] The War Powers Act of 1973, which required congressional approval to send troops into combat, is aligned with this school of thought. Therefore, the only requirement for armed forces is in defense of the homeland, and the size and structure shaped accordingly. This is the most challenging of the four concepts for military professionals because is calls for limiting the size and responsibilities of the U.S. Armed Forces. As the force downsizes, so does its capacities and capabilities, things that might be required in future operations. Although the economy will force the military to downsize, it is unlikely to see U.S. withdrawal from its alliances within the near future. Therefore, any changes within the military should consider how it would encourage international connections, thereby limiting a strictly U.S. only entanglement, during all phases of an operation.[41]

---

[38]Ibid., 336.

[39]Ibid., 337.

[40]Ibid., 184.

[41]Joint Publication 3-0, V-4; U.S. Department Of Defense. *Stability Operations*. Joint

Both the Jacksonian and Jeffersonians schools correlate with what Walter McDougall called the "old testament" of American foreign policy. This policy focused on remaining neutral in international affairs and strengthening American democracy at home.[42] One could argue that it is partly because of this old testament way American's view foreign policy that it has never created, funded, trained, or equipped a substantial force designed strictly for nation-building. However, history since World War I shows that the United States is heavily involved in international relations and nation-building operations. McDougal calls this new era after World War I the "new testament" period of spreading freedom, democracy, and international norms of human rights.[43] It is during this era that DOD is projected to operate within for the next ten years. One can argue this new testament way of thinking is the reason why the United States remained in Iraq and Afghanistan. The underlying reason the United States went to war was to secure its safety against future aggression, but staying to spread of freedom, democracy, and international norms of human rights was based on ideology. However, America struggled in its most recent attempts to achieve new testament principles in Afghanistan and Iraq. The struggle came in the

---

Publication 3-07. (Washington DC: 29 September 2011), III-1-60. Joint Publication 3-0 outlines stability tasks during all phases of an operation. Joint Publication 3-07 outlines the responsibility for Department of Defense as it pertains to stability operations; security, humanitarian assistance, economic stabilization and infrastructure, rule of law, governance and participation. Each one of these areas has a corresponding international institution in which military forces could help facilitate ties.

[42] McDougall, *The Constitutional History*, 5.

[43] Walter McDougall, *Promised Land, Crusader State: The American Encounter with the World Since 1776*, Reprinted. (Boston: Mariner Books, 1998), 10. McDougall outlines the "old testament" into four different policies: Liberty or Exceptionalism; Unilateralism or Isolationism; The American System or Monroe Doctrine; and Expansionism or Manifest Destiny. The "new testament" is divided into Progressive Imperialism; Wilsonianism or Liberal Internationalism; Containment; and Global Meliorism. McDougall argues against the policies of Liberal Internationalism and Global Meliorism citing them as wasteful and useless. However, in the *National Security Strategy-2010*, page 5, the President calls for a commitment to support human rights, democratic values, welcome new peaceful democratic movements, and support to just peace around the world.

transition between rapid combat operations in the first few months and the extended time required to achieve the political objective of creating a stable democratic government.

Mead's third school of thought is that of the Hamiltonian doctrine, which focuses on the economic primacy of the United States by linking business and trade with government institutions.[44] Government-provided security is still a requirement in order for big business to operate within international institutions. America discovered this weakness after the 11 September 2001 attack on the World Trade Center. This policy supplants international commerce as the primary means to achieve a lasting peace between nations.[45] It is the interrelationship of commerce, maybe even interdependence, that some argue makes violent aggression between those economically interconnected unlikely. War is inherently costly and damaging to both the economy and infrastructure for the nation upon whose soil the war takes place. One of the problems for the U.S. military under the Hamiltonian philosophy is that after completion of major hostilities and destruction comes the creation of interrelationships between stable governance, sustainable economy, and international institutions.

The last concept of foreign policy is that of the Wilsonians, who believe that it is America's moral obligation to spread freedom and democracy around the world.[46] The philosophy expands America's role to creating and promoting international institutions that facilitate discourse and interconnectedness. The creation of the North Atlantic Treaty Organization (NATO) and the European Union are examples of this foreign policy concept. These institutions seek to promote democracy, prevent war by finding alternative outlets, and alleviate human suffering. Amartya Sen supports the Wilsonian philosophy by pointing out that

[44]Mead, 131.

[45]Ibid., 103.

[46]Mead, 164-7.

no substantial famine has ever occurred in a democratic country regardless of the nation's wealth.[47] McDougall's counterargument aligns this Wilsonian policy with global meliorism, the idea that the world becomes better by human effort. He argues that the Wilsonian philosophy is a complete drain and waste of America's precious resource of both blood and treasure. It is illogical to attempt to instill democracy in counties whose society does not support it.[48] Despite the cost, the United States often conducts military operations to support several of these Wilsonian concepts.[49] Keeping this foreign policy philosophy in mind, any changes to America's armed forces should consider how to provide capabilities that promote rule of law, social well-being, and power sharing governments within a democracy.

Mead argues that with the end of the Cold War and the major security threat of that period now irrelevant, the rate at which American foreign policy shifts between these schools of thought has increased.[50] Currently the Jeffersonian and Jacksonian schools of thought continue to lose out against the other two when it comes to globalization and America's standing as a world leader.[51] The United States military is currently deployed to or partnered with over 130 different countries around the world. America has an exceptionally capable and robust military force, but one that is not immune to domestic economic conditions. These conditions affect how the military supports America's role as a world leader. The results of the Hamiltonian and Wilsonian polices were that they produced a large naval forces in order to expand trade markets and ensure

---

[47]Amartya Sen, *Development as Freedom* (New York: Anchor Books, 1999), 51.

[48]McDougall, *Promised Land,* 209.

[49]Recent examples of military use to support Global Meliorism concepts: Operation Tomodachi in 2011 for disaster relief; Operation Unified Response in 2010 for earthquake response; and Operation Unified Assistance in 2004 for tsunami relief.

[50]Mead, 268-70.

[51]Ibid., 269.

freedom of the seas. In essence, they created a large standing Army with a semi-projected, five-year budget that went against the original design of the United States Constitution, and enhanced the global meliorism of self-determination, nation-building, and international humanitarian aid. Regardless of which school is more prominent in today's political realm, it is the blending of all four schools of thought in which Mead details what makes American foreign policy successful.[52] Therefore, military strategy should consider each of these schools, or the blending of them, when planning the future force.

Over time, the priority of American interest has shifted between international order, security, and economic growth. Following World War II, U.S. interest focused on the creation of international systems such as the United Nations (UN), the World Bank, and the International Monetary Fund (IMF). During the Cold War, American foreign policy focused on nuclear deterrence and containment of communism while facilitating the spread of democracy and capitalism. In contrast, during the 2012 U.S. Presidential debates the political focus was on America's economic recovery and growth.[53]

It is this economic concern that is forcing the United States government, and by default the military, to develop efficient ways to achieve its political aims. With the likelihood of increased budget constraints and the uncertainty of the future threat, these different concepts will affect military strategy, which in turn requires a change to military force structure, doctrine, or training. In the *Capstone Concept for Joint Operations: Joint Force 2020*, the Chairman of the Joint Chiefs of Staff (CJCS) General (GEN) Martin Dempsey states that 80 percent of Joint Force

---

[52]Ibid., 94-6.

[53]John Avlon, "Romney on the Ropes," CNN Opinion, http://www.cnn.com/2012/10/23/opinion/opinion-roundup-third-debate/index.html?iref=allsearch (accessed 21 November 2012).

2020 is already programmed, leaving 20 percent of the force open for change.[54] He goes on to say, "The most important advancements will come through innovations in training, education, personnel management, and leadership."[55] However, doctrine and training adaptations fall outside this restriction and hypothetically can change as the situation demands. This research identifies a gap between military capabilities to conduct Phase III and its capacity to achieve peace during Phase IV.

The United States Government is capable of accomplishing a multitude of foreign policy objectives simultaneously through the application of various forms of power. Joseph S. Nye adds to the dictionary's definition of power when he states, "power is the ability to influence behavior of others to get the outcomes one wants . . . as the possession of capabilities or resources that can influence outcomes."[56] He describes three types of power within a nation. The first type for America is military power under government control that uses coercion, threats of force, or the use of force to achieve political aims.[57] Clausewitz explains military force as putting the enemy in a situation, or the threat of putting them in a situation that is worse than the alternative presented to them.[58] However, America's old testament philosophy and the need to obtain international legitimacy often restrict the employment of hard power. Hard power has obvious implications for military planners in regards to the use of force, whereas the other two forms of power may not be as restricted by these two limitations.

---

[54]U.S., Joint Chiefs of Staff, *Capstone Concept for Joint Operations: Joint Force 2020*, (Washington DC: 10 September 2012), iii.

[55]Ibid., iii.

[56]Joseph S. Nye Jr., *Soft Power: the Means to Success in World Politics* (New York: Public Affairs, 2005), 2.

[57]Ibid., 31.

[58]Clausewitz, 77.

Economic power is the second power defined by Nye. This power also uses coercion, but includes sanctions and payments as a means to alter one's behavior.[59] Diplomatic and military means can apply economic sanctions. Reversely, they can both support economic growth as with the military's involvement with micro-grants in Iraq that stimulated the local economies. In the book, *Colossus*, Niall Ferguson both divides and interrelates the control of economic power between government actions and those of international corporations.[60] America and China's economic activities in Africa are an excellent example of governmental control over corporations. The power of international corporations is one of key arguments of in Thomas L. Friedman's book, *The Lexus and the Olive Tree*.[61] The Hamiltonian doctrine supports the interrelationship between economics and the military as a way to achieve a stable peace.

The application of economic power to encourage growth becomes extremely important following Phase III operations. The difficult aspect becomes rebuilding, or in some cases building from scratch, a nation's economy destroyed during a period sanctions and major combat operations. Ideally, the World Bank, IMF, United States Agency for International Development (USAID), and DOS have the responsibility for post-conflict economic development. However, these institutions often lack the required resources and capacity to conduct such large-scale operations, and the military lacks the doctrine, education, and force structure to do it efficiently.[62]

---

[59]Nye, 31.

[60]Niall Ferguson, *Colossus: The Rise and Fall of the American Empire* (New York: Penguin Books, 2005), 15-9.

[61]Friedman, 101-12.

[62]Robert E. Litan, "The Road Ahead - How Do We Get There?" Entrepreneurship and Expeditionary Economics, http://www.kauffman.org/uploadedFiles/Enterpreneurship/ International/expeditionary-economics-summit-panel-3.pdf (accessed 18 December 2012).

Sustained economic growth requires a careful balance between the state, the market, and the society.

Soft power is the third power defined by Nye and is the main argument of his book. Soft power is the ability to get others to want what you want through attractiveness and seduction.[63] Soft power contains the Wilsonian philosophy that through American values, culture, humanitarian policies, and institutions that others will want to do what America does.[64] Nye argues that soft power is an essential means to establish globalized PMESII systems, but that it is a form of power often ignored and underfunded. Nye somewhat disregards the fact that military strength can have a certain soft power attractiveness to different cultures around the world. He analyzes the amount of dollars spent on the DOS's diplomacy for soft power versus that spent on the military for hard power. He provides a graph that shows U.S. expenditures in 2002 on public diplomacy. America spent $1.12 billion on soft power diplomacy compared against $347.9 billion spent on national defense. France was the next closest to the U.S. on soft power diplomacy expenditures. They spent $1.05 billion on soft power efforts versus $33.6 billion defense spending.[65]

The United States spends over 1,000 times more than its nearest ally on hard power versus soft power. If Mahatma Gandhi's words are true, "the spirit of democracy cannot be imposed from without. It has to come from within. The spirit of democracy is not a mechanical thing to be adjusted by abolition of forms. It requires change of the heart," then the military must contain soft power capabilities in order to assist other governmental departments efforts at achieving the political aims. Simply put, if one cannot use hard power to force a nation to accept

---

[63]Nye, 5.

[64]Ibid., 8

[65]Nye, 124.

democracy and soft power is required, then the money is either going to the wrong place or the military has to be able to apply soft power. In Iraq's case, the America military had the proper funding, but the military strategy from the previous decade did not adequately prepare the Joint Force to achieve the political goal of democracy outlined in the 2002 security strategy.

Ferguson argues that American's soft power does not extend into the areas where there is significant cultural difference. Nor does it extend into areas where political control prevents it and, therefore, is not a viable means of power. The problem arises when the United States sends its military forces into culturally different regions, such as Iraq in 2003, to change the country from a dictatorship to a democracy with only hard power capabilities. The United States military must have capabilities to project soft power since it is the largest and most visible actor during Phase III and IV operations. The military's soft power capabilities must align with the national policies and other departmental strategies of American foreign diplomacy.

The NSS is the capstone document that provides guidance on how the U.S. is to maintain continuous advantage within international diplomacy, security, information, and economics.[66] Interestingly enough, this policy contains ideas from each of the four different approaches to foreign policy and elements of all three types of powers.[67] President Barack Obama approved the latest NSS in May 2010. The strategy does not pinpoint a primary threat to the United States, but provides a list of dangers intensified by globalization. The greatest security concerns are international terrorism, spread of deadly technologies, economic upheaval, resource scarcity, and climate change.[68] The strategy outlines a strategic approach that will advance the United States'

---

[66]The National Security Strategy-2010, i-ii.

[67]Ibid., i, 1-7.

[68]Ibid., i.

national interest in four main areas: security, prosperity, values, and international order.[69] The majority of this strategy, as well as subsequent documents, continues to align American actions within the new testament schools of thought. Each one of these major areas has a subcomponent of the national strategy that is relative to military operations. More importantly for the purpose of research is how the military interprets and applies this broad strategic guidance into force structure, military programs, training, doctrine, and actions during war. Appendix D provides a diagram for how the National Security Strategy flows into the subordinate strategies used to develop the force.

In 2012, the DOD published its strategic defense review, *Sustaining U.S. Global Leadership: Priorities for the 21st Century Defense*, in order to set new priorities for the U.S. Military.[70] Even though, it was part of the DOD's defense review, the document began with the President's new strategic direction. The addition outlined five objectives: renewed U.S. long-term economic strength, requirement to preserve America's global leadership, provide security for the Nation and its allies, promote sustainable international order, and join with allies and partners to build their capacity to promote security. The President further addresses to need to end the current war in Afghanistan and reshape the Armed Forces.[71] The two-page directive from the President only partially answers why the military fights and its role in the larger governmental approach. In the rest of the directive, the SECDEF outlines in detail the current security challenges and the primary mission for the United States military.

Inside this military strategy, SECDEF Leon Panetta outlines three approaches to countering security threats: monitoring the activities of non-state threats worldwide, working with

---

[69]Ibid., v-vi.

[70]*Sustaining U.S. Global Leadership*, 1-6.

[71]Ibid., i.

allies and partners to establish control over ungoverned territories, and directly striking the most dangerous groups and individuals when necessary.[72] The document goes on to describe ten primary missions of the United States Armed Force, of which only four are relevant to this monograph: conduct counterterrorism and irregular warfare, deter and defeat aggression, provide a stabilizing presence, and conduct stability and counterinsurgency operations.[73] These primary missions describes the military's involvement in international security and stability, but only indirectly connect to other strategic directives such as renewing economic strength at home.

The overarching theme of this strategic directive for the Armed Forces is to make the U.S. and its allies safer and more prosperous at a lesser financial cost. The directive describes eight principles to shape the Armed Service for 2020 so it can economically accomplish the missions stated earlier.[74] However, should mission requirements generated from the operational environment continue to increase as currently predicted, these cost saving measures would be marginalized.[75] By combining the Presidential directive to build partner capacity with the

---

[72]Ibid.,1.

[73]Ibid., 4-6. The primary missions of the U.S. Armed Forces include 1. Counter Terrorism and Irregular; 2. Deter and Defeat Aggression; 3. Project Power Despite Anti-Access/Area Denial Challenges; 4. Counter Weapons of Mass Destruction; 5. Operate Effectively in Cyberspace and Space; 6. Maintain a Safe, Secure, and Effective Nuclear Deterrent; 7. Defend the Homeland and Provide Support to Civil Authorities; 8. Provide a Stabilizing Presence; 9. Conduct Stability and Counterinsurgency Operations; 10. Conduct Humanitarian, Disaster Relief, and Other Operations.

[74]Ibid., 6-8. The eight principles to shape the Joint Force of 2020 are: 1. Maintain a broad portfolio of military capabilities that, in the aggregate, offer versatility across the range of missions; 2. Differentiate between those investments that should be made today and those that can be deferred; 3. Maintain a ready and capable force, even as we reduce our overall capacity; 4. Reduce operating cost by reducing the rate of growth of manpower costs, minimize overhead cost, and reduce business practice cost; 5. Achieve greater utilization and efficacy with smaller force; 6. Reexamine the ratio of Active Component and Reserve Component best suited to the strategy; 7. Retain lessons of interdependence from the wars in Iraq and Afghanistan; 8. Maintain adequate industrial base and the investment in science and technology.

[75]*Joint Force 2020*, 4. "While the armed forces are likely to grow smaller, it is less likely their operational tempo will decrease."

military's approach of working with partners to establish control over ungoverned territories, one can easily see how military costs could remain status quo. One example outside the military is the DOS's foreign military sales program that financially sustains itself and aids in building partner capabilities.[76] These efforts by the DOS seek to expand partnered nation's capabilities to expand control over ungoverned spaces and protect national sovereignty. However, operations to establish democratic control over ungoverned territories tend to be relatively long term and costly if approached incorrectly.

The Defense review also emphasizes the importance of combining American efforts with its allies and partners to achieve greater control over ungoverned territories.[77] A study conducted by the Office of the Under Secretary of Defense argued that few places in the world are truly ungoverned and the real threat comes from the way spaces are governed.[78] This relates back to Wilsonian school and the need for spaces to have a democratic globalized society. For the purpose of this paper, the four primary missions of the U.S. Armed Forces bound the concept of control. A clear idea of the term *control* is necessary when considering American military

---

[76]Defense Security Cooperation Agency, "DSCA Historical Facts Book" http://www.dsca.mil/programs/biz-ops/factsbook/FiscalYearSeries-2010.pdf, 3.

[77]U.S. Department of Defense, *Dictionary of Military and Associated Terms,* Joint Publication 1-02, (Washington DC, 08 November 2010), 79. The joint publication defines control as the authority that may be less than full command exercised by a commander over part of the activities of subordinate or other organizations. However, a broader approach that includes governmental functions must be included. For the purpose of this paper, control will be defined as the ability to exercise restraint or direction over, dominate, command, with the ability to maintain a monopoly of the use of violence.

[78]U.S. Office of the Under Secretary of Defense for Policy, Deputy Assistant Secretary of Defense for Policy Planning. *Ungoverned Areas and Threats from Safe Havens,* by Robert D. Lamb, Open-File Report, U.S. Geological Survey (Washington, DC, 2008), 4-6. The report expands its definition of governance to include areas in which governments are unable to control. These areas are referred to a gaps or safe havens and include remote areas, urban areas, maritime environments, and communication networks where no one has the capacity or willingness to control. Many of these areas are outside the scope of this paper.

occupation of other countries and the limitations placed upon them during said period. Therefore, it is necessary to define control, and explain methods used to control the population during war, and sustain control during peace.

Control in this context means the ability to exercise restraint or direction, and dominate, command with the ability to maintain a monopoly on the use of violence. The level of control achieved by those in power correlates to the level of security they maintain. In his piece, *"The Logic of Violence in Civil War,"* Stathis Kalyvas outlines several different methods to gain control and the following benefits once control is achieved.[79] His hypothesis is that during wartime, "the higher the level of control exercised by a political actor in an area, the higher the level of civilian collaboration with this political actor will be."[80] Both Adolf Hitler and Saddam Hussein used security forces as a means to enforce control over the population. However, once U.S. forces destroyed the Iraqi military, there was no longer a means to maintain control. The limited coalition troop presence left the Iraqi society open to post-conflict looting, murder, and chaos.

Violence as a means of coercion is a method to gain control during war, but it connects to how someone applies violence and the means in which it is applied that enables control. The rules for the use of force during war are less restrictive than those during peacetime occupation. Force or the threat of it is often necessary to defeat the enemy and maintain control of the population during combat. This is not always the case during counterinsurgencies or irregular warfare operations.

---

[79]Stathis N. Kalyvas, *The Logic of Violence in Civil War* (New York: Cambridge University Press, 2006), 111-45.

[80]Ibid., 111.

There is often a higher level of violence during Phase III. Therefore, people are more likely to abide by rules laid down by those who are applying violence. However, after completion of hostilities, the use of violence cannot be the only means of maintaining control and security, especially in a counterinsurgency operation. According to a 2007 RAND study, security is the first priority when transitioning from combat to stability operations.[81] Kalyvas explains that during the stability period control and collaboration become self-reinforcing. His theory of control interconnects politics with military/security forces and the social structure.

Although Kalyvas's book focuses on civil war, the theory is applicable to American peace-enforcement/peacekeeping operations in Bosnia and Kosovo as well as counterinsurgency operations in Afghanistan and Iraq. The Army adopted several aspects of this theory in its Field Manual 3-24, *Counterinsurgency*. The doctrinal publication is a guide on how to balance the use of force with other measures to gain and maintain control.[82] American political and military leaders weigh the cost to gain and maintain control against the resources required. Additionally, they look to establish systems within the host nation to sustain control as they seek to transition operations to civil authority.

Systems Theory: Interconnectedness, PMESII, and Operational Shock

Systems are a part of everyday life. Their existence ranges from as small as living cells and molecules to as large as complex systems of international relations. Scientists, strategists, theorists, and planners alike study systems. For the military planner, the study of these systems attempts to provide clarity during the uncertainty of war and the aftermath that follows. The

---

[81]James Dobbins et al., *The Beginner's Guide to Nation-Building* (Santa Monica, CA: Rand Publishing, 2007), xxiii.

[82]U.S. Department of the Army, *Counterinsurgency Operations,* Field Manual 3-24, (Washington DC, December 2006).

theory behind interconnected complex adaptive systems helps to explain the complexity in transitioning from Phase III to Phase IV operations. Understanding this theory allows one to analyze how destroying a certain piece of infrastructure may affect other variables within the political, social, and economic constructs. Therefore, it is necessary to both define a system in context to this discussion as well as narrow its scope to military application.

The DOD defines as systems as, "a functionally, physically, and/or behaviorally related group of regularly interacting or interdependent elements; that group of elements forming a unified whole."[83] Although this definition is helpful, Robert Jervis provides a more detailed definition. His definition highlights the relationships between and within systems, "(a) A set of units or elements is interconnected so that changes in some elements or their relations produce changes in other parts of the system, and (b) the entire system exhibits properties and behaviors that are different from those of the parts."[84] The first part of this definition is self-explanatory, but the second part may not be so easy to understand within a military context. An example is the different branches within the military that perform different functions apart from the military as a whole. Society often views the military as a system that uses hard power to force others to do its will. However, Civil Affairs and Medical Corps are branches within the military system that often help to facilitate the application of soft power.

After defining what a system is, Jervis goes on to provide a way to understand a system. He states, "A systems approach shows how individual actors following simple and uncoordinated strategies can produce aggregate behavior that is complex and ordered, although not necessarily predictable and stable."[85] Understanding the different relationships between systems aids staff

---

[83] Joint Publication 3-0, GL-17.

[84] Jervis, 6.

[85] Ibid., 7.

officers in the military planning process when determining what aspects of a system to target. However, planners cannot indiscriminately target aspects of any one system during Phase III without understanding what losses will be sustained in Phase IV.

Joint Publication 3-0, *Operations* outlines a system perspective approach as a way to think of the operations environment as interacting systems of political, military, economic, social, information, and infrastructure.[86] Appendix E provides a diagram to help understand this interconnected operational environment. The difficulty for planners is to understand how these systems interact and how to predict what any change to one system will have on another. The internal and external links connecting the systems cause the complexity described by Jervis.

In Douglass North's article, "Institutions," he points out that institutions place constraints on systems and create additional complexity both within and between systems. He defines institutions as, "humanly devised constraints that structure political, economic, and social interaction."[87] Luckily, there are methods, although not guaranteed, to achieve the desired goal to help comprehend the complexity of systems. Peter Senge provides two fundamental ways of seeing a system: seeing patterns of interdependency, and seeing into the future.[88] Systems diagrams are one of the tools to help planners see patterns of interdependency. In order to see into the future, planners must start with a thorough understanding of the present systems. The Army design methodology is a process to aid in understanding, visualizing and describing complex

---

[86]Joint Publication 3-0, IV-4, 5.

[87]Douglass C. North, "Institutions," *Journal of Economic Perspectives*, Issue no. 1 (Winter), 1991, pp. 97.

[88]Senge, 343.

situations.[89] A focused or detailed look at one system will help explain the interconnectedness inside and between each of the different PMESII systems.

A detailed breakdown of the social system within the PMESII framework illustrates the interrelationship between the systems. In Jamshid Gharajedaghi's book, *Systems Thinking*, he describes the dimensions identified within the multi-minded social system. The first dimension he describes is the generation of *wealth* and its distribution within society.[90] The distribution of wealth within a society determines who feasts and who suffers famine. Given Sen's statement that famine does not occur in democracies, then the application of soft power to achieve freedom should be easy. Adding to this argument is the work of Minxin Pei, where he finds that democracies that reach a per capita income (PCI) measured in purchasing power parity or *PPP* between $2,001 and $3,000 have a democratic life expectancy of 26 years. Democracies that reach a PCI above $6,000 acquire immortality.[91] One can see why creating democratic governments have such a strong backing when combining Friedman's idea that democracies do not fight each other, Sen's conclusion that democracies do not experience famine, and Pei findings that democracies exceeding a PCI above $6,000 become immortal. A combination of the three together creates a middle class that is peaceful, stable, and economically prosperous. However, democracies and dictatorships are not the only two forms of governmental options.

Karl Marx considered wealth as an aspect of the economy, which in turn formulated the underlying causes of social realities. Through Marx's viewpoint, it is easy to see how wealth links

---

[89]U.S. Department of the Army, *Operations*. Army Doctrine Publication 3-0, (Washington, DC: Department of the Army, 11 October 2011), 1-9.

[90]Gharajedaghi, 56.

[91]Minxin Pei, "Economic Institutions, Democracy, and Development," http://www.carnegieendowment.org/1999/02/26/economic-institutions-democracy-and-development/3i9 (accessed 18 December 2012).

social system with economic and political systems. Marx went even further by interrelating economic and social systems with the political system, which formed the Communist government of Russia in the early nineteenth century. Communism interrelates all three systems, so if a given military destroys the Communist government during Phase III operations, they essentially destroy the other two systems connected to it.

Gharajedaghi also linked the social system to three other systems within the PMESII framework: the generation and dissemination of (social) *truth* within a society links to the system of information; the formation and institutionalization of (social) *values* intertwines both economic and political systems; and development and duplication of (social) *power* can arguably interrelate with political, military, and economic systems.[92] The problem for planners revolves around the fact that they must be able to defeat the enemy without severely, unintentionally disrupting or destroying interconnected PMESII systems.

The implication of these interrelationships is the unpredictability of how a change in one node or variable of the social system not only affects that system, but the other five systems connected to it.[93] These side effects, as doctors call them, could have a positive and/or negative impact on other PMESII systems. Complex systems have a dense collection of interconnected units, nodes, variables, or institutions that create difficulty in tracing or predicting the impact of any change to a system.[94] It would then seem logical to break the system down into different parts in order to understand the system as a whole. However, Jervis points out planners cannot

---

[92]Gharajedaghi, 56.

[93]Joint Publication 3-0, GL-17. Joint Publication 3-0 defines node as, "a location in a mobility system where a movement requirement is originated, processed for onward movement, or terminated (JP 3-17), and as an element of a system that represents a person, place, or physical thing."

[94]North, 97.

understand the system by simply observing its individual parts; a term he calls *reductionism*.[95] It is this comprehensive approach to systems in which military planners approach operations to achieve both their national and military strategic objectives.

For the purposes of this research, there are two theories as to how systems operate. Chaos theory describes how systems with deterministic behavior (having determined outcomes) sometimes produce widely diverging outcomes, making deterministic systems ironically unpredictable. Chaos theory is outside the scope of this paper. The second theory is that of complexity. Complexity is defined by the interaction between variables or nodes that affect the overall system. The amount of complexity depends on the type and number of connections. Systems can exhibit complexity, chaos, or a combination of both depending on the system, the nodes and the variables involved against the outcome it produces.[96]

In his book, *In Pursuit of Military Excellence*, Shimon Naveh develops a systems approach for military actions at the operational level.[97] The approach applies to what Ludwig von Bertalanffy describes as *open systems*, "a system which exchanges energy with the outside environment from both import and export methods."[98] Given this description, it is clear that PMESII are all open systems because they are human constructs that interact with one another through both importing and exporting. Gharajedaghi adds that the actions of each one of these

---

[95]Jervis, 13.

[96]Gharajedaghi, 92-93.

[97]Shimon Naveh, *In Pursuit of Military Excellence: The Evolution of Operational Theory* (Portland: Frank Cass, 1997), 23.

[98]Ludwig V. Bertalanffy, *General Systems Theory* (New York, 1975), 38. Bertalanffy describes both closed and open systems. A closed system does not interact with the environment outside the system itself, it has a limited purpose, and has a predetermined output. However, for the focus of this paper, Bertalanffy's theory of open systems is used.

systems aim to achieve a certain purpose.[99] It is often the purpose of the system in which the military planner seeks change.

According to Naveh, systems have two types of feedback, which he calls positive and negative feedback.[100] Positive feedback is input into the system from the outside environment. Negative feedback is the systems resistance to or adaptation from the outside environment. Negative feedback within a system is what creates side effects. These side effects could become positive feedback into other systems because of the two systems interconnectedness. This interconnectedness creates complexity for military planners trying to target one aspect of a system without causing side effects to another.

The Naveh approach focuses on the military system. He outlines three different methods to affect the military system through an approach he calls, "operational shock."[101] The purpose of operational shock is to overload a system causing it to disintegrate or collapse, essentially preventing it from achieving its original aim.[102] Naveh's second method to achieve operational shock involves concurrent operations to inject positive feedback across the opponent's depth by simultaneously engaging the front and rear areas of the system.[103] Although, Naveh focuses on military-against-military operations, the United States often seeks much larger objectives than just the destruction of the advisory's military capabilities. More recently, the American purpose

---

[99]Gharajedaghi, 33-8.

[100]Naveh, 16.

[101]Ibid., 16-19. The first method is achieved through conducting a penetration of the enemy's outer defenses, penetrating in depth, and disrupting the cohesion between the various nodes within the military system. The third method is massing forces on the center of gravity, which prevents the system from achieving its original aim.

[102]Ibid., 15-7.

[103]Ibid., 18.

for war is often to alter the adversary's political system to align closer with American national interest, not to destroy all the systems within a nation. Numerous American military operations between the end of World War II and Libya in 2011 resulted in changes to multiple systems. However, not all of them were intentional.[104] Therefore, it is necessary to place Naveh's operational shock theory into the larger political context and overall purpose for the war. In addition, planners have to consider what shocking the military system has on the adversary's other systems.

The NATO operation in Libya is a classic example of interconnected systems. The destruction of Omar Kadafi's military forces enabled the resistant movement to overthrow his regime, demonstrating the interconnectedness between political, military, and social systems. This was the intended purpose of the operation. However, an unintended side effect to the conflict affected Libya's economic system. Libya's oil exports suffered severely for seven months following the conflict.[105] At a critical time when the new fledgling interim-government needed new revenue, Libya's main source of income was declining. Expanding this side effect globally to oil prices was Libya's membership in Organization of Petroleum Exporting Countries (OPEC) and Libya's position as the largest proven oil reserves in Africa.[106] A third side effect to destroying Kadafi's control was a decrease in regional stability. Tuareg tribesman, who previously served in Gadhafi's military, returned home to Mali, formed a separatist group called

___

[104]Since WW II, the threat of or actual employment of American military forces has directly or indirectly resulted in regime changes during WW II Germany, Japan, France, Italy, and Austria; the undesired outcome of Vietnam in 1975; Thailand in 1962; Grenada in 1983; Panama in 1989; Nicaragua in 1990; Haiti and Bosnia in 1995; Kosovo in 1999; Afghanistan in 2001; Iraq in 2003; and Libya in 2011.

[105]U.S. Energy Information Administration. "Libya." http://www.eia.gov/cabs/libya/pdf.pdf (accessed 27 November 2012).

[106]Ibid., 1-3.

the National Movement for the Liberation of Azawad (MNLA), and began a military campaign to separate the northern region of Mali from governmental control.[107]

It is this interconnectedness or complexity between the systems that creates what Senge calls "creative tension."[108] This tension is the gap between the political vision for what America wants the future to look like and the reality of the current situation. Planners must understand the level and type of positive input, the system it is directed toward, and the length of time that input is necessary to achieve the vision. Creative tension for military leaders rests at the operational level of war. The Joint Publication defines the operational level as "the level of war at which campaigns and major operations are planned, conducted, and sustained to achieve strategic objectives within theaters or other operational areas."[109] This tension creates the discourse between strategists on what to destroy during Phase III and what to rebuild during Phase IV.

Globalization as the Ultimate Complex System

One of the first concepts the NSS points out is how globalization has intensified security threats. The concept of globalization is critical to understand in order to grasp the interconnectedness of governance, economics, military, social, information and infrastructure systems. Globalization vastly increases the complexity of transitioning from Phase III to Phase IV operations. Phase III operations often destroy stabilizing political institutions and global economic ties, as portrayed in Figure 1. Planners must consider how replacing a regime in Phase

---

[107]Scott Stewart, "Mali Besieged by Fighters Fleeing Libya," STRATFOR Global Intelligence, http://www.stratfor.com/weekly/mali-besieged-fighters-fleeing-libya (accessed 27 November 2012).

[108]Senge, 139-44. Naveh also describes a similar concept of cognitive tension as it applies to the operational level of war. Within this context, he describes it as the dichotomy required to preserve a controlled disequilibrium between the national strategy and the tactical mission.

[109]Joint Publication 3-0, *Operations*, GL-14.

III nullifies or voids all binding agreements held by that regime. The challenge during the transition period and into Phase IV is not only establishing a new government capable of internal governance, but also connection to globalized institutions such as the United Nations, World Bank, and International Monetary Fund.

These interconnected globalized systems may not be present inside the country prior to U.S. involvement. Alternatively, destruction of the systems may be an intentional act as part of a combined military strategy. Regardless of these aspects, many theorists believe that globalization and institution building are what achieves lasting peace.[110] The effort to establish globalized institutions, build various institutions of control, and achieve sustainable peace is what concerns military planners during Phase IV and Phase V.

Thomas Friedman explains the theory of globalization in that it connects politics, the environment, transportation technologies, geopolitics, social aspects, and economics within each country.[111] He outlines how they interact with every other globalized country around the world.[112] A simple example of the interconnectedness and the side effects is that of a reusable, cloth Wal-Mart bag. Wal-Mart sells the reusable bag in America with the words, "Wal-Mart: Save money. Live better," printed on the outside. The bag appeals to American interest in both saving money and saving the environment by using the same bag every time an individual shops. However, China manufactured the bag and shipped it to America, incorporating the interest of the oil industry by using fuel in its manufacture and transportation. Environmentalists argue that the side

---

[110]Friedman, 248-50. In his book, Friedman credits the French philosopher Montesquieu with creating an international "Grand Republic," which connected reciprocal dependency of two nations based off trade. He later explains British writer Norman Angell's theory that no two industrialized nations would go to war because the destruction would outweigh the benefits for both winner and loser.

[111]Ibid., 248.

[112]Ibid., 248.

effect of burning fossil fuels to create electricity in Chinese coal plants to produce the bag and then shipping the bag increases global warming. This example helps explain interconnectedness and side effects, but it does not help explain the driving force behind globalization.

Ferguson calls the American Empire the political counterpart to economic globalization. He states, "If economic openness – free trade, free labor movement and free capital flows – helps growth, and if capital is more likely to be formed where the rule of law exists and government is not corrupt, then it is important to establish not only how economic activity becomes globalized but also – by what mechanism – economically benign institutions can spread around the world."[113] In many ways, the National Security Strategy subscribes to this theory. Economic openness is a way to create greater global stability. Ferguson's theory bases on the assumption that it is too socially and economically costly to go to war with other interconnected globalized nations.

It is because of this connectivity that nations tend to solve their problems through peaceful means in order to maintain economic development and prosperity. Friedman's conflict deterrence theory assumes that by connecting politics, environment, geopolitics, and economics within every country around the world that it would achieve a lasting peace. He states, "No two countries that both had McDonald's had fought a war against each other since each got its McDonald's."[114] However, he excludes civil wars and border skirmishes, which are many of the peacekeeping operations the UN finds itself involved in today. There is a current international discourse over the security impact of globalization. In some ways, the war between Georgia and Russia in 2008 proved the theory wrong since both countries possessed a McDonald's. This

---

[113]Ferguson, 184.

[114]Friedman, 232.

conflict also partially negates other popular theorists, like Thomas Barnett, in regards to the link between globalization and peace.

Thomas Barnett's book, *The Pentagon's New Map* combines security, economic, political, and culture factors to help predict the future areas of war and peace. His argument integrates the works of Thomas Friedman and Samuel Huntington.[115] Barnett combined these two different concepts onto a geographical map to help focus strategist's efforts in identifying future conflict regions around the world. The map divides the world into two basic categories, one with conflict and one without war.

The first category he described is the "functioning core," also referred to as *the core*, which is an interconnected globalized area where future peace is likely.[116] The second category is an area of future conflict called the "non-integrating gap," also referred to as *the gap*. The gap is an area with thin connections to the outside world, both institutionally and technologically.[117] Barnett states that inside the gap, all wars, civil wars, ethnic cleansing, genocide, mass raping, employment of child soldiers, all UN peacekeeping operations, and all recent U.S. nation-building operations take place.[118] A recent predictive study conducted by the U.S. Army TRADOC Intelligence Support Activity (TRISA) supports Barnett's conclusion about potential

---

[115]Barnett, *The Pentagon's New Map*, 51.

[116]Friedman, 248-50. In his book, Friedman credits the French philosopher Montesquieu with creating an international "Grand Republic," which connected reciprocal dependency of two nations based off trade. He later explains British writer Norman Angell theory that no two industrialized nations would go to war because the destruction would outweigh the economic benefits for both winner and loser.

[117]Samuel P. Huntington, *The Clash of Civilizations and the Remaking of World Order* (New York: Simon & Schuster, 1998), 68, 185. Huntington argues that certain civilizations will resist globalization through violent means based on their cultural beliefs.

[118]Thomas P.M. Barnett, "National Security Strategy" (lecture, National Defense University, Fort McNair, Washington DC, 18 August 2006), http://www.c-spanvideo.org/program/193938-1 (accessed 3 December 2012).

for continued conflict in the gap. According to TRISA's forecast, nine of the top ten areas that could require the employment of a brigade combat team are located inside the gap.[119]

There is remarkably little debate between commentators in regard to conflict in the non-integrating gap, except to the conflict between Russia and Georgia. Besides this conflict, many of Barnett's critics focus on his futuristic view of peace within the core and the inevitability of worldwide globalization. The first group of critics use Thucydides's claim that nations fight wars over fear, honor, and interest.[120] Globalization may cover the reasons of fear and interest, but honor within social cultures is likely to remain a reason for war. A legitimate argument is that Russia sought to protect its honor by inflicting revenge on Georgia for the death of the Russian peacekeepers in South Ossetia.

The second argument of critics target Barnett's claim that all gap countries can be globalized. Jared Diamond argues a different point in that economic expansion and technology evolved from environmental conditions.[121] Although nations in these certain geographic regions could advance technologically with cell phones and the Internet, it does not automatically equate to the development of industrial and financial institutions that interconnect economies. Barnett's theory rests on the establishment of external economic connections that raise the cost of war so high that war itself is generally avoided. He argues that without these institutions, conflict will continue.

---

[119]U.S. Army TRADOC G2, TRADOC Intelligence Support Activity – Threats, *TRISA's Top 10 Potential Operational Environments*, (Fort Leavenworth, Kansas, 30 January 2012) , 12.

[120]Thucydides, Melian Dialogue, available at: www.hks.harvard.edu/organizing/tools/ Files/melians.pdf (accessed 2 December 2012), 3.

[121]Jared Diamond, *Guns, Germs and Steel*, 2nd ed. 5 vols. (New York, New York: W.W. Norton and Company, Inc., 2001).

Barnett counter argues that globalization will happen through a combined effort of multiple nations over a period of several generations, but acknowledges certain periods of conflict are inescapable before getting there. He realized from his Russian studies that it took over 40 years for the U.S. to achieve economic defeat of the Soviet Union. He attributed this defeat to the ideas of free market capitalist.[122] The second true victory Barnett claims is in facilitating China's co-optation to market economics shortly thereafter.[123] His argues that similar free market capitalists searching for cheaper labor and raw materials will eventually push globalization to nations inside the gap. Barnett acknowledges that America cannot do it unilaterally. He states, "While America must lead the effort, it is going to be Asia doing the heavy lifting on the ground. Chinese and Indian entrepreneurs are simply more used to investing in places with bad infrastructure, weak governments, and inhospitable climates."[124] However, this combined economic globalization effort requires new national strategies from the United States, China, and India.

Freidman also discusses a country's willingness to accept aspects of a globalized society, which interlinks nations to achieve peace. He argues that in order for a nation to prosper they must accept what he calls "the golden straitjacket" of a globalized political-economic environment.[125] He states that it is up to that society to choose to accept these principles for

---

[122]Thomas P.M. Barnett, *Great Powers: America and the World After Bush* (New York: Berkley Trade, 2010), 112-3, 229-30.

[123]Ibid., 145-147.

[124]James Joyner, "America and the World After Bush: Economics and Globalization," New Atlanticist, http://www.acus.org/new_atlanticist/america-and-world-after-bush-economics-and-globalization (accessed 3 December 2012).

[125]Freidman, 105.

economic prosperity, appealing to a Jacksonian school for foreign policy.[126] Although it is a

nation's choice, Samuel Huntington accuses globalization of exacerbating civilizational, societal,

and ethnic self-consciousness to point where it could cause conflict.[127]

Summary

Military leaders have substantial input as to what the Joint Force of 2020 will look like

and its employment. However, they do not control the strategic objective of current and future

mission. American political leaders are the ones who make these decisions. Since the end of the

Cold War, the U.S. has led multinational military interventions in multiple different countries for

a variety of different reasons. If political objectives were known in advance, clearly defined, and

remained constant it would amplify military proficiency. However, the sheer number of

unknowns caused by side effects from interconnected systems negates this utopia for military

planners.

The political objectives causing U.S. military involvement change before, during, and

after the war. National sentiment, international legitimacy, and economic crisis shift political

objectives over time. The discourse between new testament and old testament schools for

American foreign policy continues to affect the military and operational strategies. The argument

centers around the amount of hard power positive feedback required to win a war followed with

the amount of soft power necessary to sustain the peace and create lasting stability. Which side of

the debate one subscribes to will determine what means are built for the military to employ.

The NSS is the guiding document in which the military bases its strategy. The NSS

prescribes future objectives of American security, prosperity, values, and international order. The

---

[126]Ibid., 108-9.

[127]Huntington, 68, 185.

specific military strategy outlined by the SECDEF includes countering terrorism, deterring and defeating aggression, providing stabilizing presence, and conducting stability and counterinsurgency operations. These objectives are similar to that of other globalized societies. According to a 2007 RAND study, military operations that include nation building have become increasingly longer in duration, lasting between five to ten years.[128] Both national and military leaders look for ways to create stabilizing institutions within systems that build a stable environment with minimal cost to the United States.

The complexities of a globalized system make achieving political goals of freedom and expanding democracy a challenge for military planners. The links between the American PMESII framework and similar frameworks within the International community and targeted entity enhance creative tension for military leadership. The difference is between knowing that any change to one node has side effects on other nodes,and knowing the exact change or changes needed for each node to achieve the desired objective. Military decision makers should keep these concepts in mind when developing the force of 2020 to ensure it has the capabilities and capacity to defeat the enemy during war, but also to rebuild the required institutions for sustained peace afterwards.

WORLD WAR II AND IRAQ CASE STUDIES

During World War II and the 2003 Iraq War, the United States used its military force as a means of diplomacy. The strategic aim behind both missions was to replace a brutal totalitarian leader and with a democratic government. During Phase III, the United States military destroyed certain aspects of the German and Iraqi military, political, and social structure in order to achieve its objective. After winning each war, America transitioned to a long period of Phase IV stability

---

[128]Dobbins, *The Beginner's Guide*, iv.

operations. Each war offers unique insights into the impacts that Phase III had on follow on operations.

World War II – European Theater

National Security Strategy

The United States underwent a drastic change in its social, economic, and geopolitical status between World War I and the end of World War II. By the end of 1919, many American turned inward and reverted to what McDougall defined as old testament principles of isolation and avoidance of international entanglements. Although the United States did not have a comprehensive National Security Strategy like the ones published today, it did have similar policies that guided its foreign relations. The reigning idea in the 1930s was to stay home and protect the United States within its borders. One approach was to stay out of international entanglements that might drag the United States into war. Presidential policies focused on America's economic growth and expansion. American's foreign policy relied heavily on what Nye describes as soft power. Several policies promoted domestic programs aimed at achieving American self-reliance.[129] Congress shaped these beliefs and passed safeguards against foreign political and economic entanglements that might drag the United States into another war.

The Great Depression in the 1930s hit the United States extremely hard. Americans were no longer willing or had the means to intervene in world events such as the Japanese conquest of Manchuria in 1931 or Germany's invasion of Czechoslovakia in 1938.[130] The United States went so far as to sign the Kellogg-Briand Pact, a policy that outlawed war as a way to achieve a

---

[129]Herring, 484.

[130]Ibid., 491-98, 513.

political end in 1927.[131] For most of 1930, the nation continued to downsize the Army while only slightly increasing the Navy. This action reflected the basic principle of the Jeffersonian policy as described by Mead of protecting America's borders. In August 1935, Congress passed a neutrality act that forbade the sale of arms to belligerents. As much as 95 percent of the American population supported policies that kept America out of foreign affairs. Members of organizations such as Veterans of Future Wars demanded compensation of $1,000 per man so they could enjoy life before being killed in battle.[132]

Early on in his Presidency, Franklin Roosevelt supported and even introduced many of these neutrality policies. Even though, the majority of the country held isolationist views, President Franklin Roosevelt remained aware of the problems facing Western Europe in the late 1930s. He became keenly aware of the political situation in Europe as Germany began to rise to power. Hitler's aggressive and expansionary tactics began to worry members of the League of Nations. The League pushed for greater U.S. involvement, but without avail. It was not until Hitler's annexation of the Sudeten region of Czechoslovakia in 1938 that Roosevelt began to have a change of mind towards possible war.[133] By this time, the British and French had less than a year to mobilize for war. President Roosevelt started to have similar thoughts about preparing for war, but in order to take action, he first had to win an uphill battle against national sentiment and Congressional legislation.

Historians debate whether Hitler's rise to power would have been possible without the global Great Depression of the 1930s. While much of the world struggled in economic despair in

---

[131]Michael R. Matheny, *Carrying the War to the Enemy: American Operational Art to 1945* (Norman, OK: Univ of Oklahoma Pr (Trd), 2011), 46.

[132]Charles DeBenedetti, *The Peace Reform in American History* (Bloomington, IN., 1980), 122-33.

[133]Herring, 513.

1933, Nazi Germany under Hitler was beginning its ascent into an industrial powerhouse. In the six years between 1933 and 1939, Hitler withdrew from the Treaty of Versailles, created a strong sense of nationalism, reoccupied the Rhineland, and began an industrial rearmament program that set Europe on the path to war.[134] Hitler forged alliances with Japan, Italy, and even Russia for a short period as he prepared to expand Germany's "living space" across Europe. In doing so, Hitler was able to create what Naveh and Dietrich Dörner describe as a well-buffered system that could sustain itself through six years of total war.[135] Because Hitler exerted extensive political control of the civilian population, he was able to manipulate the country into war. This interconnection between political and social control is how Kalyvas explains the logic behind government sanctioned violence.[136] As Hitler's power and control expanded, so did Roosevelt's concerns about preparing for war.

By late 1939, President Roosevelt began to seek alternatives to the isolationist policies enacted over the past decades. He was able to push through a "peace bill" that lifted the arms embargo to belligerents.[137] As Hitler begins his invasion of France, Roosevelt secured a $10.5 billion dollar rearmament program to increase the size of the Army and Navy.[138] With the help of Roosevelt, Secretary of War Henry L. Stimson pushed the Selective Service Act of 1940 through

---

[134]Colin S. Gray, *War, Peace and International Relations: an Introduction to Strategic History* (London: Routledge, 2007), 129-33.

[135]Naveh, 4-18. Also see Dietrich Dorner, *The Logic of Failure: Recognizing and Avoiding Error in Complex Situations* (Reading, MA.: Basic Books, 1997), 74-6. Although they do not apply their theories directly to case studies in World War II, the idea behind well buffered systems is that they are resistant to positive feedback. These systems are able to withstand large amounts of input and still manage to maintain their intended purpose.

[136] Kalyvas, 111-14.

[137]Herring, 519.

[138]Ibid., 520.

Congress, creating a conscript army without a declaration of war.[139] In addition to his political agenda, President Roosevelt sought out American's support for the war through a comprehensive propaganda campaign.

With the American population set on neutrality and isolation, President Roosevelt knew he needed to prepare America's social system for total war. Many American's believed that if the United States were to become involved in Europe, it would lead to bigger government, the dismantling of New Deal reforms, and a crackdown on civil liberties. These concerns were secondary to the concern that a war would cause economic hardship and produce high causalities.[140] Although Jervis's theory on interconnections between different parts a system had yet to be published, Roosevelt understood the interconnection between politics, social concerns, and information campaigns. To address these social concerns, Roosevelt created the Office of Government Reports, the Division of Information at the Emergency Office of Emergency Management, and the Coordinator of Information.[141] These agencies missions were to prepare the American civilian population for war. The propaganda machine sought to explain the American way of life. It took large-scale global problems and translated into how they would affect each individual's life.

As President Roosevelt prepared the nation for war, the Department of War was preparing for a fight on two fronts. To get a complete understanding of the military strategy used to prepare for the war, one must look at the period between the wars. There was an abundance of military innovation during the interwar period between World War I and World War II, much of

---

[139]Robert K. Griffith Jr., *The U.S. Army's Transition to the All-Volunteer Force 1968-1974* (Center for Military History, United States Army, Washington, DC, 1997), 7.

[140]Susan A. Brewer, *Why America Fights: Patriotism and War Propaganda from the Philippines to Iraq* (New York: Oxford University Press, USA, 2009), 91.

[141]Brewer, 93.

which is outside the scope of this study. The concept of strategic bombing and industrial

mobilization were key ideas used to develop the operational strategy.

Similar to the lack of a comprehensive national security strategy, there was no national

military or national defense strategy that guided the Department of War from 1918 to 1940. Each

Service developed systems across the DOTMLPF framework that met their service's needs. The

Army focused on combined arms warfare with emphasis on mechanized cavalry.[142] The Army

Air Corps devolved around the theories of French GEN Giulio Douhet and American BG William

Mitchell. Douhet's theory of using air power to destroy interconnected systems became the

precise essence of the Allied strategic bombing campaign against Germany. The five targeted

systems were industry, transport infrastructure, communications, government, and the will of the

people.[143] Military officers studying at professional military education centers learned each of the

innovations relevant to their fields. The Army built the Combined General Staff College at Fort

Leavenworth in 1922 to teach these ideas and concepts to those officers selected to attend.[144] In

addition to teaching new theories, the College developed new doctrine and procedures for

implementation across the Army.[145]

Another lesson that American military leaders learned from World War I and nurtured

during this period was the requirement to mobilize private industry. The Army established the

Industrial College in 1924, which focused on wartime procurement and mobilization procedures.

---

[142]Alexander M. Bielakowski, "Mechanization in the Interwar U.S. Cavalry." Excerpt from *U.S. Army Cavalry Officers and the Issue of Mechanization*, 1916-1940. PhD diss., Kansas State University, 2002. 1-13.

[143]Giulio Douhet, "Aerial Warfare," *The Command of the Air*, USAF Warrior Studies, Washington, DC, Office of Air Force History, 1983, 1-8.

[144]Matheny, 46-8.

[145]Ibid., 48-9.

Officer studies centered on the requirement to mobilize national industry during times of war. The mobilization of the entire nation was necessary if the Allies hoped to be successful during World War II.

Approach to and Action in Combat

In the two years prior to 1941, the American military and political systems began to prepare for war. The expansion of Japanese Empire in the Pacific Ocean and the Nazi Germany in Europe gave President Roosevelt great cause for alarm. He understood the lessons from World War I and the concept behind total war.[146] Roosevelt knew that political flag waving would not be enough to win the war, and he needed the resources of the entire nation in order to achieve the political aim. Millions of people must serve; fight in battle; produce war materials; ration and conserve precious resources; and eventually raise funding by buying war bounds.[147] The lifting of the arms embargo and direct support to the British and French set the United States on a path to total war with Nazi Germany.

The Japanese attacks on Pearl Harbor on 7 December 1941, coupled with Hitler's declaration of war, brought the United States into a two-front war. America had multiple allies on both the Pacific and European Fronts. Even before the United States entered the war, Roosevelt sought to build a forum that would promote political discourse between nations. In 1939, he supported Under Secretary of State Sumner Welles's plan to create an international organization

---

[146]Carl von Clausewitz discusses the difference between total war and limited war. He describes total war as, "an act of force, and there is no logical limit to the application of that force. Each side, therefore, compels its opponent to follow suit; a reciprocal action is started which must lead, in theory, to extremes." Clausewitz then goes on to bound war by stating, "the political object, which was the original motive, must become an essential factor in the equation. The smaller the penalty you demand from your opponent, the less you can expect him to try to deny it to you; the smaller the effort he makes, the less you need to make yourself," thus limit war is achieved. Clausewitz, 78-81.

[147]Brewer, 88.

that later became the UN.[148] These alliances would prove both indispensable during the war and extremely tenacious during the stability phase.

The U.S. entered the war aligned with the Allied Powers of Great Britain and the USSR. America's first strategic decision was to make the European Theater its first priority.[149] The United States' initial plan was to launch a cross-channel, amphibious assault from Great Britain into German-occupied positions in northern France. The Russians needed to open a second front against the Axis powers on the European continent in order to force Hitler to fight on two fronts. However, due to the slow mobilization process, American planners did not believe the cross-channel invasion was possible until 1943 or 1944. As Collin Gray pointed out, war is waged by logistics.[150] Even with the efforts of the Industrial College, it would take another three years before American industry could exceed the demand for war materials. Knowing that a land force would take time, planners turned their focus toward air power. American and British governments wanted to conduct direct strikes against the German war machine as quickly as possible, and air power was the means to accomplish the task.

America's involvement for the first two years of the war centered around logistical buildup and attriting the German military. As Litan's theory describes, a nation must first have the means, resources, and capacity in order to achieve their political ends. In 1941, America was only beginning to develop the military means and the political ends to the war. It was not until the Allied conference in Casablanca in January 1943 that Roosevelt stated that the political aim was

---

[148]James Dobbins, *After the War: Nation-Building from FDR to George W. Bush* (Santa Monica, CA: Rand Publishing, 2008), 15.

[149]Matheny, 160.

[150]Gray, 131.

the unconditional surrender of the Axis powers.[151] Although America's goals after the war would far exceed that of just a defeated Germany, their first task was to destroy the Nazi system.

During the first two years of the war, the Allies attempted an air interdiction campaign against the German industrial web to cripple its economy with the expectation that it would have side effects on the social and political unity to continue to the war.[152] The idea was basic system theory to inject overwhelming positive feedback into a system until the entire system collapses. However, this early campaign proved to be ineffective due to a lack of available means used against a well-buffered German economic system. As more resources became available and the Allies achieved air superiority, the Allied forces shifted their operational strategy in accordance with Douhet's principles.

The next plan was to destroy specific German industry involved in making war materials. The bombing concept aimed to destroy the industrial capacity, but once again, Germany was able to apply enough negative feedback to balance the system.[153] The temporary shock created by the bombing campaign was not enough to collapse the system. The next step in the air offensive was to target the will of the German people. This campaign lasted until just before the end of the war. By mid-1944, Allied bombers had achieved air superiority over Germany and were bombing all five of Douhet's prescribed targets. Arguably, the Allied bombing of logistical transportation hubs proved to have the greatest impact.[154] By May 1945, Allied bombers dropped over 1.3 million tons of bombs, destroyed 40 percent of the urban areas inside seven of Germany's largest

---

[151]G. John Ikenberry, *After Victory: Institutions, Strategic Restraint, and the Rebuilding of Order After Major Wars* (Princeton: Princeton University Press, 2001), 169.

[152]Robert A. Pape, *Bombing to Win: Air Power and Coercion in War* (Ithaca, N.Y.: Cornell University Press, 1996), 256-9.

[153]Robert A. Pape, 256-9.

[154]Ibid., 276.

cities, and killed over 305,000 civilians.[155] Although the bombing campaign alone did not cause the collapse of the Nazi system, it did have a significant impact on post-war reconstruction.[156]

As Allied land forces crossed into Germany in the fall of 1944, the German system began to collapse under the combined weight of Allied airpower, naval, and ground forces working in concert. As the Americans captured each town, they assumed control of government and economic systems. The German political, economic, and military systems continued to collapse as Allied forces moved closer to the capital. Berlin was the main objective, because therein lay the ultimate prize of Adolf Hitler.

Robert Pape and Colin Gray both make the argument that Hitler was the center of gravity for Nazi Germany.[157] Hitler's control of the political and social systems kept Germany fighting through the spring of 1945, even after it was clear to everyone involved that Germany would lose the war. Shortly after the death of Hitler, Nazi Germany would agree to an unconditional surrender. Unlike the end of World War I, by the end of this war the Allies achieved complete annihilation of the German political, social, and military systems.[158]

Many historians state that World War II was only a continuation of an unfinished war that started 25 years earlier. They claim that the Treaty of Versailles placed too many demands on an undefeated German nation. German military officers claimed that their political leaders betrayed them by signing the Armistice.[159] Because most of the fighting took place in France, the

---

[155]Ibid., 254.

[156]Ibid., 254.

[157]Pape, 283-9; Gray, 129.

[158]Gray, 99-102.

[159]Herring, 503, 519.

German social, economic, and infrastructure systems remained untouched. This was not the case by the end of World War II in 1945.

Throughout the war, Allied forces were slowly destroying Germany's PMESII capacity. During the war from 1942 until 1945, the Allies devastated the German military machine and then abolished it completely shortly after the end of the war. The social system felt not only the impact of both military and civilian casualties, but also the psychological effects from the strategic bombings and losing the war. In addition, the social system had to absorb an extreme influx of over ten million German-speaking refugees from Eastern Europe. The Russians, French, British, and Americans occupied Germany and controlled their internal politics. Under the legacy of the shelved Morgenthau Plan, German economy suffered through a five-year period of industrial disarmament.[160] This is the transition point, as shown on Figure 1, that efforts to destroy the enemy's systems shift toward rebuilding host nation control and capacity.

Transition to Stability

By the summer of 1944, America's strategic aims for the end of the war became clear: unconditional surrender of the Nazi Party; full occupation of Germany by Allied forces; complete denazification of the government; the establishment of an open democratic system; dismantlement of the German military and industrial war capabilities; and a reeducation of the German citizen.[161] However, America's grand strategy expanded beyond just their involvement in Germany. The United States sought to remove spheres of influence and create an environment of mutual security throughout Europe.[162] Adverse to post-war planning himself, President Roosevelt

---

[160]Dobbins, *After the War*, 19.

[161]Pape, 257.

[162]Ikenberry, 174.

established a series of interagency committees to address post war issues. As early as 1941, Roosevelt was committed to long-term occupation of German and the reconstruction of Germany. In order to meet his aims, he employed a whole-government approach to handle post war responsibilities.

Both the President and the military understood the terms of unconditional surrender. The approach was to create a military organization designed to handle stability operations. In August of 1942, the Army established a Military Government Division under the new Office of the Provost Marshal General.[163] A little over a year later on 4 May 1943, the Army established the new Civil Affairs Division under the command of Major General (MG) John Hilldring. Civil Affairs officers filled these billets with the responsibility to translate each governmental department's grand strategy into tactical operations.[164] These officers received training on non-military aspects of whatever the Army needed them to do.[165] Several other non-military agencies prepared guides to aid in civil affairs training and implementation. Agencies such as the Economic Institutions Staff, Office of Strategic Services, and the Department of Agriculture produced over 70 guides to aid Civil Affairs Officers.[166]

The first post-war challenge was to address the new political order after the collapse of the Nazi regime. Allies argued that one of their most critical objectives was "the preparation for an eventual reconstruction of German political life on a democratic basis."[167] The military needed

---

[163]Dobbins, *After the War*, 18.

[164]Ibid., 17-19.

[165]Ibid., 17.

[166]Ibid., 19.

[167]James Dobbins and Rollie Lal, *America's Role in Nation-Building: from Germany to Iraq* (Santa Monica, CA: RAND Corporation, 2003), 15.

officers trained in political and economic affairs to maintain control and run the country. This was one of the missions of the Civil Affairs officer. As American ground forces captured various German cities during the eastward movement to Berlin, military government units took over administration of German territory. In March 1945, there were over 150 military government units operating throughout Germany. The goal of these detachment units was to instill democracy. They started with holding elections at the "grass roots" in the smaller local cities and towns.[168] Between 1945 and 1950, the military would slowly transition political control back over to a heavily supervised German government.

The second challenge in post war Germany was to reestablish its social structure. By the spring of 1945, Allied forces achieved a troop level of one soldier to every ten German civilians.[169] Although this force dropped significantly in the following two years, it remained large enough to maintain stability in the country.[170] The mission of the Military Government Units was to reinstate rule of law and reintegration of the German refugees. In the fall of 1945, the United States established a constabulary force to oversee legal matters until a German police force stood up. This force coupled with occupation troops maintained a high enough degree of security allow other government and reconstruction programs to go unhindered. One argument is that without this high level of security and rule of law, economic and political progress would not have been possible.

Reinvigorating the German economy was the third challenge facing military leaders in Germany after the war. Reconstruction plans varied between France, Britain, and the United

---

[168]Dobbins, *After the War*, 28.

[169]Dobbins and Rollie Lal, *America's Role in Nation-Building: from Germany to Iraq*, xvii.

[170]Ibid., 9-15.

States. Reconstruction plans conflicted even between the United States governmental departments. Military planners drafted the *Handbook for Military Government in Germany*, which outlined a soft approach to restoration.[171] The Secretary of Treasury Henry Morgenthau called for a more hard line approach that sought to prevent Germany from starting World War III. However, military governors like GEN Lucius D. Clay pushed the reconstruction effort forward because of the threat from communist Russia and pressure to reduce the financial aid to German.[172] These two aspects created a greater aim for the United States besides just operations within Germany.

Dolman describes pure strategy as placing oneself in a position of greater advantage, and that is exactly what Roosevelt articulated in the 1941 Atlantic Charter.[173] In G. John Ikenberry's book, *After Victory*, the aim was to "lock the democracies into an open, multilateral economic order jointly managed through new institutional mechanisms."[174] This idea combines North's and Kalyvas' theories about institution building to maintain control and security with Barnett's interconnection of globalization. As the war continued on, the United States became stronger and took on a larger leadership role in global affairs. By the end of the war in 1945, America generated 50 percent of the world's GDP.

As early as 1939, President Roosevelt's ideas of an open economic system with Europe were already taking root in policies like the lend-lease program. At the start of the program, the British were eager to sign it in order to receive military equipment during the war. After America became involved in the war, differences arose between the British and American trade policies.

---

[171]Dobbins, *After the War*, 19.

[172]Ibid., 19.

[173]Dolman, 6.

[174]Ikenberry, 165.

58

Article 7 of the Lend-Lease agreement stipulated that neither country would restrict trade that each would reduce current trade barriers, and eliminate preferential duties.[175] This was just one example of how American foreign policy promoted interconnectivity and interdependence between countries.

America continued to push for binding institutions it felt would decrease chances of another world war. America increased its ties with Europe with the creation of the NATO. The purpose of this organization was to promote collective security through mutually supporting political and military policies. These binding institutions of political, military, and economic policies served the United States as the Cold War began to unfold. By 1950, the NATO contained 13 member-nations and the UN had 60. These institutions created not only a platform for international discourse, but also an organization capable of taking action during times of crisis.

Iraq War 2003

National Security Strategy

The Office of the President of the United States published the 2002 U.S. NSS with the hindsight of the 11 September 2001 attack on the United States, and the anthrax scare the following week. This grand strategy coupled with President Bush's policies shaped the military's approach to the war in Iraq. President George W. Bush's opening sentence in the NSS concluded that freedom, democracy, and free enterprise were the only sustainable model for national success.[176] He went on to state, "These values of freedom are right and true for every person, in every society—and the duty of protecting these values against their enemies is the common

---

[175]Ibid., 188.

[176]Office of the President, *The National Security Strategy of the United States of America* (Washington, DC: The White House, September 2002), iii.

calling of freedom-loving people across the globe and across the ages."[177] The statement

capitalized on Freidman, Sen, and Pei's ideas that democracies are stable, peaceful, support their

population, and provide economic growth for all parties involved. These Wilsonian concepts lay

the moral foundation for American action against tyrant regimes. Although President Bush

appealed in policy circles to the Jeffersonians, he expounded on the idea that America must strike

first in order to maintain its security.

In the NSS, President Bush went on to address the dangers of foreign governments that

harbor and support terrorism. He prescribed action through the utilization of the best intelligence

and then proceeding with deliberation. He stated, "History will judge harshly those who saw

coming danger but failed to act."[178] President Bush was referring to weapons of mass destruction,

both nuclear weapons and chemical weapons, used on the civilian population through terrorist

attacks. In his view, action is the only means to secure peace and security. History is unclear

whether President Bush was referring directly to Iraq in regards to action at this point, but

immediately following the 9/11 attacks President Bush pushed to find any bit of intelligence

linking Saddam to the attacks. Even without direct intelligence or evidence of a connection from

Iraq to 9/11 attacks, President Bush initiated war planning for regime change for Iraq in

November 2001.[179]

Section VI of the NSS details the benefits of economic globalization. It promotes

institutions that govern trade regulations, tax policies, provides rule of law, and investments in

health and education.[180] This section of the United States' grand strategy to support globalization

---

[177]Ibid., iii.

[178]The National Security Strategy-2002, iii.

[179]Herring, 945.

[180]The National Security Strategy-2002, 21-3.

targets non-globalized economies around the world. This section coincides with Sen's argument that national security and economic growth depend on interconnected systems of political, social, economic, information and infrastructure.[181]

Section VII of the NSS focuses on opening societies and building the institutions of democracy. The strategy outlines the requirements needed to receive economic assistance from the United States. American efforts seek to enhance the effectiveness of the World Bank by expanding grants and student loans.[182] It also discusses providing medical resources to counter HIV/AIDS, emphasizing preventative health education, and providing agricultural development aid. This grand strategy addresses funding and products for economic development, but does little to address the force requirements needed to accomplish the stated goals.

Although the grand strategy on paper was clear, President George W. Bush and SECDEF Donald Rumsfeld took a different approach to the war in Iraq. Both individuals believed that a small, light, highly mobile, and lethal military force could quickly win any war. Following combat operations, a new democratic government would assume control of the country within three months. They somehow overlooked or missed the fact that industrialized economic democracies, established through the rule of law that are interconnected to the globalized network cannot be created in a three-month period.

A second issue is that the American military strategy and governmental systems did not address or prepare the American society for long-term stability operations and long deployments overseas. The requirements were outlined in the 2002 National Security Strategy. Ferguson makes the argument that most American executives, educated elites, as well as military forces

---

[181]Sen, 53.

[182]The National Security Strategy-2002, 21-3.25-8.

tend to prefer working from home unlike America's British counterparts.[183] One could reason that McDougall's new testament approach to America's foreign affairs is acceptable as long as the government does not require its citizens to go anywhere for extended periods of time. This concept is arguably one of the reasons why President Bush opposed concepts like nation building and the long-term occupation of Iraq even before the war began.[184] The difficulty with where American citizens' work is as much of a problem as how the government spends its money in regards to foreign policy. Nye would argue that American expenditures on hard power in Iraq vastly outweighed soft power diplomacy efforts to achieve peace.

The military strategy when American invaded Iraq in 2003 was remarkably similar to the military strategy in place before the Gulf War in 1991. The idea was that the U.S. Joint Military Force converges to deter and defeat an enemy force on the battlefield. Interestingly, the majority of the requirement for land-based operations falls within the Army's domain. This force structure design places most of the burden of occupying a country after war on the Army. Similar to the Joint Force, the U.S. Army in 2003 was designed, equipped, trained, and focused mainly to conduct the major combat operations. The Army's 2001 *Field Manual 3-0, Operations*, described the Army's war fighting focus to include full spectrum operations during war, conflict, and peace.[185] However, only two mission tasks come out of the three paragraphs that define the role of the Army during peacetime: prepare all aspects of the DOTMLPF for war, and help shape the international security environment through peacetime military engagements. The military strategy

---

[183]Ferguson, 202.

[184]Michael R. Gordon and Bernard E. Trainor, *Cobra II: the Inside Story of the Invasion and Occupation of Iraq* (New York: Pantheon, 2006), 3-5.

[185]U.S. Department of the Army, *Operations*, Field Manual 3-0 (Washington, DC: Department of the Army, 14 June 2001), 1-3. This manual was the capstone guide to military operations during the 2003 war in Iraq. There are several updates to the manual since this one was published.

from 1991 to 2003 designed a force during peace that limited the planner's operational strategy to fighting the war in Iraq in such a way that it did not facilitate the transition to stability.

Approach to and Action in Combat

Although the Iraqi war did not start until 2003, global application of hard power against Iraq started 13 years earlier. These actions degraded the systems within Iraq that hindered rapid reconstruction during Phase IV. Iraq's invasion of Kuwait led to UN-imposed economic sanctions against Iraq on 6 August 1990, Operation Desert Storm in 17 January 1991, and Operation Desert Fox in December 1998. For the most part, these hard power sanctions remained in effect until Saddam's fall in 2003. The sanctions were part of an economic power approach under the UN Security Council Resolution 687 to force Saddam to remove or dismantle weapons of mass destruction (WMD) capabilities. However, Saddam's defiance against allowing weapons inspectors into country resulted in American and British air strikes against suspected Iraqi WMD facilities under an operation code name Operation Desert Fox. The operation in December 1998 consisted of a four-day bombardment of 415 cruise missiles and over 600 bombs. In addition to the military operations, the UN sanctions took a devastating toll on Iraq's social system.

In September 2000, the Office of the United Nations High Commissioner for Human Rights (OHCHR) released a report detailing the effects of sanctions on the Iraqi people. During the period between 1990 and 2000, the maternal and infant mortality rate rose, hospitals and health centers deteriorated, and the illiteracy rate rose.[186] The World Bank's country brief on Iraq added infrastructure and institutional degradation to the list.[187] These sanctions were in place

---

[186]Office of the High Commissioner for Human Rights, "The Human Rights Impact of Economic Sanctions On Iraq," Campaign Against Sanctions on Iraq, http://www.casi.org.uk/info/undocs/sanct31.pdf (accessed 29 November 2012), 4.

[187]World Bank, "Iraq Country Brief," http://web.worldbank.org/WBSITE/EXTERNAL/COUNTRIES/MENAEXT/IRAQEXTN/0,menuPK:313115..pagePK:141132..piPK:141107..theS

because of Saddam's refusal to comply with United Nation's mandates. The connection between international sanctions and systems degradation in Iraq further demonstrate the interconnection between systems and the effects that the restriction of globalization have on to a nation. The sanctions coupled with Saddam's war against Iran bankrupted the country. Iraq was still on the decline in 2003 when the Americans and British launched military operations. After receiving the notification for war, the Ba'athist party began to destroy certain governmental ministries to further hinder any coalition reconstruction effort after the war. It would be the responsibility of the military to reverse this governmental, economic, and infrastructure decline of Iraq during Phase IV operations.

Niall Ferguson and others outlined the reasons why the United States opted for war as a means of diplomacy in Iraq.[188] First was that Iraq failed to comply with UNSC 687 and 1441. The second reason was that Saddam was a tyrant and was inflicting human suffering as demonstrated by the chemical weapons attack on the Kurdish population. The third reason was the need to send a message to the rest of the Middle East concerning the new war on terrorism. The fourth reason was to establish democracy in Iraq in hopes it would spread throughout the Middle East. The final reason was to create bases in Iraq and pull American forces out of Saudi Arabia.[189] Expediting the decision was a belief that the international sanctions on Iraq were going to collapse due to French, Chinese, and Russian pressure.

These six reasons held little support outside a select group of America's allies. Unlike America's involvement in World War II, the war in Iraq consisted of an exceedingly small coalition of international supporters. President Bush used his most trusted international diplomat,

---

itePK:313105,00.html (accessed 29 November 2012).

[188]Ferguson, 156

[189]Ibid., 156. Also see; Gordon and Trainor, 3-7.

Secretary of State Colin Powell, in a failed attempt to gain additional supporters for the war in Iraq during a UN visit.[190] The aim of the Iraq war was to remove Saddam from power, prevent Iraq from acquiring weapons of mass destruction, and free the Iraqi people. In order to accomplish these aims, military planners assumed that portions of Saddam's military force must be destroyed during Phase III operations. The planners, empowered by Rumsfeld, also assumed that Phase IV would only last approximately three months. Then, during Phase IV, the Office for Reconstruction and Humanitarian Assistance (ORHA) would hand control over to the Interim Iraqi Administration. This is further evidence of the lack of synchronized planning for Phase IV because the military plan backed an anti-Saddam insurgent group led by Ahmed Chalabi.[191] Although this simplistic plan was the one used during the invasion, an early plan called for a longer occupation period and much higher troop levels.

In 1998, as the Commander and Chief of the United States Central Command, (CENTCOM) GEN Anthony Zinni developed CENTCOM OPLAN 1003-98 for operations in Iraq that required a minimum of 385,000 Soldiers, while other estimates were as high as 450,000.[192] Zinni based the assessment off a detailed analysis of Iraq's PMESII systems. He feared that a collapse in Saddam's regime would lead to further fragmentation of the nation's social system along ethnic lines. A fear shared by both the Jordanians and Kuwaitis.[193] Secretary of State Collin Powell, the Army Chief of Staff GEN Eric Shinseki and, initially, GEN Tommy Franks shared the belief that a considerable number of Soldiers would be required for the operation. However, neither the administration nor the SECDEF shared these views. The

---

[190]Ricks, 90-94.

[191]Gordon and Trainor, 107, 315-7.

[192]Ibid., 24-7

[193]Ibid., 27-8.

President and SECDEF believed that with less than 125,000 troops over a six-month period the Americans could easily win the war.[194]

By the time, the invasion launched on 20 March 2003, the total military force including allies numbered around 175,000. The force ratio in Germany after World War II was one American Soldier per every ten civilians.[195] These troop levels allowed the allied forces to maintain control after the fall of the Nazi regime and establish a military government detachment as they moved through each new area.[196] Conversely, in Iraq, the ratio was one coalition soldier for every 150 civilians. This troop level prevented the Army from maintaining control of the population after the fall of the Ba'athist Party. The fall of the Iraq regime and collapse of the other institutional systems validated all aspects of Kalyvas's theory on control over a civilian population.

The SECDEF and GEN Franks continued to negotiate the number of troops needed to win the war and those needed for follow-on operations. In the end, the SECDEF won, and GEN Franks promised a "shock and awe" campaign in Iraq with the troops levels that were authorized. The promised campaign achieved military victory in a short amount of time with an extremely small military force. It also promised to rapidly transition from Phase III to Phase V civil control in under three months, allocating only a short period for Phase IV. The important aspect to understand is that, unlike World War II, only two other Army Divisions had deployment orders to support follow-on operations. The troop strength in Germany built up over a four-year period to achieve the 1:10 ratio, whereas in Iraq, the plan assumed that the same Divisions could progress

---

[194]Gordon and Trainor, 4-7.

[195]Dobbins, *After the War*, xiii.

[196]Department of the Army, "WWII - European-African-Middle Eastern Theater," Center for Military History, http://www.history.army.mil/books/wwii/Occ-GY/ch12.htm (accessed 18 December 2012).

from Phase II to Phase V in less than six months. During 2003, the ratio of Soldier to civilian would not exceed 1:125. Military planners did adjust some planning considerations in order to mitigate the discrepancies in smaller troop levels and the occupation requirement afterwards.

Unlike the Allied bombing campaign in Germany during World War II, most of Iraq's infrastructure was off limits for targeting purposes. This policy spared the oil refineries, electrical, and transportation systems from destruction by U.S. forces. However, complexity theory shows that changes in one node create side effects on the other nodes and systems. Coalition forces did not destroy the critical infrastructure directly. The destruction of the regime coupled with the coalition's inability to maintain control of the population devastated the infrastructure.

The purpose of the war was to change the Iraqi government system, specifically to remove Saddam from power. The military achieved this purpose within the first month of the war. By April 15, several military leaders believed the war was over.[197] Franks directed military planners to begin focusing on redeployment operations instead of intensive stability requirements. Rumsfeld even went so far as to cancel follow-on forces, namely the 1st Cavalry Division, which was set to deploy on April 21.[198] Keeping the interactions between nodes in mind, the changeover of political systems focused on Baghdad alone. Planners put little consideration into governmental control at the provincial and district levels. Secretary of State Condoleezza Rice stated, "The concept was that we would defeat the army, but the institutions would hold everything from the ministries to the police force."[199] In other words, Iraq's military system would be destroyed, but the political, social, and economic systems would hold. However, the goal of the United States' grand strategy was to replace the Iraqi political system. With the

---

[197] Gordon and Trainor, 459.

[198] Ibid., 461.

[199] Michael R. Gordon, "The Strategy to Secure Iraq Did Not Foresee a 2nd War," *New York Times* 19 October 2004.

collapse of the military and the fall of Saddam, the absence of an absolute sovereign power began to negatively affect the other systems in Iraq.

The Iraqi Army went from a force of over 150,000 Soldiers before the war to fully dissolved afterwards. In addition to the loss of personnel, Allied forces destroyed much of the Iraqi Army's Soviet equipment. This limited Iraq's ability to use its military forces to assist with security operations for the post war. Army Field Manual (FM) 3-24, *Counterinsurgency*, highlights the importance of Host Nation security forces to establish control, a security force that American pressure caused to dissolve.[200] In addition, the destruction of the Ba'athist government function provided by Ministry of Interior caused many of the Iraqi police forces to quit reporting to work. With the absence of security and loss of control, coupled with the fact Saddam released all prisoners prior to the war, looting of critical infrastructure sites became rampant. Criminal looting drastically reduced essential services within Baghdad. Looters stripped precious metals from electrical facilities, sewage treatment, and water plants. Electricity shortages caused looting to increase in Baghdad. Although coalition forces did not directly target power plants, unintended destruction of fuel lines and electrical lines running to and from the power stations further decreased electrical output. This is the transition point as shown in Figure 1 where host nation control and capacity was at its lowest point. Destruction caused by coalition forces began to decrease, and priority should have shifted to "shock and awe" stability operations.

As the security situation and essential services continued to decrease, coalition attempts to inform the public were negligible. Bombing raids destroyed phone networks, television, and radio networks in order limit Saddam's ability to communicate with his military forces, the same systems that coalition forces needed to communicate with the Iraqi people.[201] Although, the

---

[200]U.S. Department of the Army, *Counterinsurgency*, 5-1.

[201]Gordon and Trainor, 472-3.

Phase III destruction of Saddam's communication system aided in rapid defeat of the enemy

force, it also prevented the Director of the Office for Reconstruction and Humanitarian Assistance

(ORHA), Jay Garner's team, from communication with the local population in during Phase

IV.[202] In the same manner, the new government could not communicate its actions and progress

to its people. The only information that the Iraqis received was what they saw happening around

them, the degradation of essential services that the new government was supposed to provide.

With the wrong type of feedback going into the Iraq social system, an insurgent growth became

the side effect. The insurgency continued to grow, and the situation in Iraq continued to decrease

over the next four years because of the inefficiencies of all three levels of strategy.

There was other positive feedback going into the system that targeted other systems

besides communication. The amount of force placed on the Iraqi security forces caused them to

dissolve shortly after the dominate phase ended. This dissolution negated any possibility of their

use in the security effort during the stability phase.[203] Still, one could not conceive that the

transition process between Phase III and Phase IV would be so difficult since the Soldiers were

already in place and the DOD was in charge of post-conflict operations, but it was.[204]

Transition to Stability

Minimal planning went into Phase IV for Iraq from both the DOS and the DOD because

of President Bush's and the SECDEF dislike for nation-building operations. Their influence on

---

[202]Ibid., 472-3.

[203]Ibid., 459-465.

[204]This would be the first time since World War II that the Department of Defense led post-conflict operations. Secretary of Defense Donald Rumsfeld believed that the Department of State and USAID were already overwhelmed with ongoing operations in the Balkans and Afghanistan. Therefore, DOD spent minimal effort on synchronizing interagency efforts towards Phase IV operations. In addition, see Dobbins, *After the War, 105.*

the remainder of the Executive Branch was apparent by the lack of organized interagency planning teams for stability operations. Although Phase II and III planning began almost immediately after 9/11, GEN Franks did not begin planning for Phase IV until October 2002. The post-conflict command structure was unknown until the President made the decision for DOD to lead the effort in December 2002. The Secretary of State believed that the military had both the resources and the manpower to lead Phase IV operations, and did not object to the President's decision.[205] Even though the military had the money and personnel, it did not have the experience needed to rebuild globalized institutions of governance, economics, and rule of law. The National and military strategies in 2002 did not prepare a force across the DOTMPL framework to interconnect these various systems with security efforts to create a comprehensive stability plan.

By February 2003, GEN Frank's planning staff concluded, "The campaign would produce conditions at odds with meeting the strategic objectives" established by the National Strategy.[206] Some of the main concerns for Lieutenant General (LTG) David McKiernan's planners were control of the borders, key infrastructure to be protected, and the allocation of resources to establish post-war control throughout Iraq.[207] Interestingly, none of these concerns dealt with the establishment of a functioning democracy, providing humanitarian assistance, creating economic stability, or establishing and enforcing rule of law.[208] However, planners were

---

[205205]Dobbins, *After the War*, 107.

[206]Ibid., 105.

[207]Ibid., 105.

[208]Joint Publication 3-07, III-2. These are the stability operations functions as listed in the Joint Publication 3-07. Also see U.S. Department of the Army, *Stability Operations*, Field Manual 3-07 (Washington, DC: Department of the Army, October 2008), Chapter 1.

unable to convince GEN McKiernan or GEN Franks to change their "shock and awe" operational plan so shortly before initiating Phase III operations.[209]

Although not in the lead for post-conflict operations, the DOS began planning for Phase IV in the fall of 2002. The government attempted to establish several, small interagency groups to conduct Phase IV planning and war-gaming at the National Security Council level. However, these committees did little to synchronize the plans between Phase III Dominate Operations and their impacts on Phase IV.[210] Several governmental agencies independently planned Phase IV operations without knowing what systems the military planned to destroy in Phase III. The interconnectedness of these systems makes unilateral planning ineffective. Had the military decided to destroy the Iraqi oil infrastructure in Phase III as they did in WWII, those actions would have significantly impacted DOS's actions during Phase IV in regards to revenue generation and infrastructure repair. This was especially significant since Iraq's main source of income was oil revenue, money that the State Department intended to use to rebuild the country.

As Condoleezza Rice stated, "the concept was that we would defeat the army, but the institutions would hold everything from ministries to police forces."[211] It does not take a complete understanding of globalization or systems theory to understand cause and effect relationships. The plan failed to account for the fact that when a tyrant-emplaced government is defeated, a power struggle, especially within an ethnically divided society, will soon follow.

---

[209]LTC Steven W. Peterson, "Central But Inadequate: The Application of Theory in Operation Iraqi Freedom," http://www.dtic.mil/cgi-bin/GetTRDoc?AD=ada441663&Location= U2&doc=GetTRDoc.pdf (accessed 18 December 2012), 10-1. Also see Gordon and Trainor, 146.

[210]Dobbins, *After the War*, 107.

[211]Michael R. Gordon, "Catastrophic Success: The Strategy to Secure Iraq Did Not Foresee a 2nd War," New York Times, 19 October 2004, http://www.nytimes.com/2004/10/19/international/19war.html?_r=0 (accessed 18 December 2012).

The lack of concern and interagency planning for Phase IV operations became apparent when the security situation in Baghdad began to deteriorate in April 2003. Jay Garner led the stability effort under the ORHA for Iraq. After a string of perceived failures, Ambassador Paul Bremer replaced him on 16 May 2003 and established the Coalition Provisional Authority (CPA) for Iraqi occupation. The CPA was an ad hoc organization without any of the constructs of basic organizational theory. Adding to the problem were DOS employees refusing to deploy to Iraq due to security concerns. Many of those who deployed, rotated out every 90 days proving Ferguson's idea that Americans do not like to work abroad.[212] Without a cohesive interagency team or a comprehensive Phase IV strategy, Bremer implemented a de-ba'athification policy and directive to dissolve all Iraqi national security ministries and military formation. These actions further decreased the Allies' ability to maintain control over the various interconnected systems.

There was no unified command for Civ-Mil operations in Iraq, even though both Bremer and the new military commander, LTG Rick Sanchez, both worked for the SECDEF. Rumsfeld retained the decision-making authority back in Washington instead of at a headquarters in Iraq.[213] The command structure between operations in Iraq, the DOD, the DOS, and the NSC remained disjointed for those two years. This lack of unified effort supports critics' assertions that Phase IV was a disaster. Even though the DOD was in the lead during both Phase III and Phase IV operations, it failed to find ways that translated tactical actions into strategic success. The military DOTMLPF structure in 2003 focused on conducting Phase III operations. There was little desire by DOD and DOS to jointly analyze and understand interconnected PMESII systems, and what expertise it would take to establish those systems in a foreign country.

---

[212]Dobbins, *After the War,* 114, 121.

[213]Ibid., 122.

Summary

The United States entered World War II without a comprehensive National Security Strategy and subordinate Defense Strategies as we think of them today. However, President Roosevelt understood the requirement to prepare the nation's political, social, and industrial systems for war. His preparation captured the essence of Count Helmuth von Moltke's statement, "even a single error in the original assembly of the armies can hardly ever be made good again during the entire course of the campaign."[214] After the United States declared war, it began the systematic destruction of German systems. Allies started with a strategic bombing campaign, and then switched to occupying land forces. These land forces were trained and prepared to conduct a long intensive occupation period that would eventually return Germany to a powerful ally during the Cold War.

The United States' National Security Strategy in 2003 encompassed many of the Wilsonian principles such as freedom and democracy. President Bush stated the purpose of the Iraq war was, "to disarm Iraq of weapons of mass destruction, to end Saddam Hussein's support for terrorism, and to free the Iraqi people."[215] The Iraqi social, economic, and industrial systems were in rapid decline due to years of war, UN sanctions, and general neglect. However, planners somehow overlooked these interconnected systems. Within the United States, President Bush did little to prepare the American people for the long nation-building effort that followed. Planners deluded themselves into believing that a democratic Iraq was achievable in less than three months. The United States did not enact Hamiltonian ideas of binding institutions to create

---

[214]Helmuth von Moltke, *Moltke On the Art of War: Selected Writings* (New York: Presidio Press, 1995), 91.

[215]George Bush, "President Discusses Beginning of Operation Iraqi Freedom," The White House, http://georgewbush-whitehouse.archives.gov/news/ releases/2003/03/20030322. html (accessed 7 March 2013).

interdependence and collective security throughout the region. The disbandment of the military and exile of the Ba'athist party after the war caused the entire Iraqi system to collapse. Rebuilding these systems was the focus of the military for the next seven years.

CONCLUSIONS AND RECOMMENDATIONS

The United States' Grand Strategy remains engrained in the new testament philosophy described by McDougall. The 2010 National Security Strategy expands America's role to promote security, prosperity, values, and international order.[216] The DOD aligns its military strategy with the NSS and includes objectives to counter terrorism and irregular warfare, deter and defeat aggression, provide a stabilizing presence, and to conduct stability and counterinsurgency operations.[217]. In order to achieve these desires, one must understand the various systems and institutions that create collective security. Globalization is the ultimate complex system that creates economic interconnectedness to achieve economic growth. [218] American involvement in the Philippines between 1898 and 1934 spanned Phases II through Phase V. Either by happenstance or by design, the United States used similar approaches to operations during World War II and in Iraq. In each of these cases, America's grand strategy was to transition control to a democratic nation with similar economic institutions friendly to the United States. During Phase III, the military both intentionally and unintentionally destroyed political, military, and social systems only to rebuild those systems during Phase IV.

---

[216]The National Security Strategy-2010, v-vi.

[217]Sustaining U.S. Global Leadership, 4-6.

[218]Mead, 27-28.

Rebuilding of Destroyed System

A guest speaker for the Command and General Staff College said that America does not do well in nation-building operations because they are harder than simply winning a military victory.[219] He cited recent examples to create democracies in Iraq, Afghanistan, and Kosovo. However, during World War II, the United States employed an interagency effort to successfully implement its nation-building strategy. A 2003 RAND study on nation-building operations during World War II concluded that democracy can be transferred and societies can change under the right set of circumstances.[220] Thomas Barnett argues that by creating a *systems administration force*, the United States is capable of conducting successful nation-building operations.[221] This theory is strengthened when combined with Nye's argument on the allocation of resources between hard power and soft power. GEN Dempsey stated that 20 percent of Joint Force 2020 is open for change.[222] Twenty percent of DOD's 1.2 million people and annual budget of over $400 billion allows the United States military significant opportunity to become more efficient in its ability to create globalized systems during and after war that achieve lasting stability.

World War II, like any war, produced a unique set of circumstances that challenged post war stability operations. A 2008 RAND study outlined the circumstances that ended Phase III operations in Germany with the unconditional surrender by the government, devastating defeat of the military, highly advanced economies, and a homogenous society.[223] However, studies found

---

[219]Anonymous, 2012.

[220]Dobbins and Lal, *America's Role in Nation-Building*, 20.

[221]Thomas P.M. Barnett, *Blueprint for Action: A Future Worth Creating* (New York: Berkley Trade, 2006), xix.

[222]Joint Force 2020, iii.

[223]Dobbins, *After the War*, 35.

that only one or two of these conditions are present in subsequent U.S. Phase IV stability operations. Although all of the circumstances in Germany are significant by themselves, the study minimizes the interrelation between all four systems: governance, military, economic, and social. The United States foreign policy sought to tie each of these systems together, not only within Germany, but also throughout Europe and America itself, immersing its foreign policy in Wilsonian philosophy. In addition to the changes created inside Germany, there was an increase in the global strength of the United States at the end of the war. The level of commitment that America was willing to expand, coupled with its rise in power, enabled its achievement of success.

Phase III operations in Iraq ended with a different set of circumstance. There was no formal surrender by Saddam Hussein. Iraq did not have an advanced economy, and what economy it had was deteriorating under UN sanctions. Sunni, Shia, and Kurdish lines divided Iraqi's social system. In addition to the different conditions between Iraq and Germany, the United States was different from what it had been in 1945. America no longer held 50 percent of the world's GDP. In 2003, it held military and political commitments around the world to include an ongoing war in Afghanistan and peacekeeping mission in Kosovo. War planning for Iraq focused on winning the war, which it did magnificently. However, it failed miserably at winning the peace. Rumsfeld issued planning guidance for the war in Iraq that resembled the Jeffersonian philosophy. The idea was to protect America by defeating its enemies abroad with the smallest force possible and bringing the force back home as quickly as possible. Nation-building operations dragged the U.S. further down, not necessarily militarily but arguably though loss of political capital and economic decline.

The argument here is not to claim that there was no post war planning for Iraq. Jay Garner claimed that the DOS, DOD, Treasury, USAID, and even the Department of Agriculture each had a post-war plan.[224] The problem was that there was not a synchronized interagency approach toward achieving the strategic aim. Unlike World War II, exceedingly little consideration went into creating new stabilizing institutions, regional or international, to interconnect Iraq with the rest of the world. This may have been due to what Francis Fukuyama describes as the lack of overall coordinated effort across the U.S. Government.[225]

One can easily see from Iraq that the U.S. government did not have the capability within a single governmental agency or department of achieving "shock and awe" for stability operations at the start Phase IV operations. Starting war planning with less than a year before execution does not allow significant time to bring five different government agencies together. It certainly does not allow time to form a synchronized and cohesive interagency organization set on achieving America's strategic aim. Although these interagency problems are well documented, they still hinder U.S. operations.[226] Therefore, the military must adapt its DOTMLPF structure in such a way that it is capable of achieving a "shock and awe" effect within Phase III and during the first six months of Phase IV. Although rarely in today's operations is there a clean and clear transition between the phases. However, sometime within the first six months of Phase IV the local population must see improvements in their quality of life; otherwise they may turn against their liberators, which could cause the American public to turn against its civilian decision makers.

---

[224]Dobbins, *After the War*, 130.

[225]Francis Fukuyama, ed., *Nation-Building: Beyond Afghanistan and Iraq* (Baltimore: The Johns Hopkins University Press, 2006), 8-9.

[226]Lesley A. Warner "Capacity Building Key to AFRICOM's Mission," *World Politics Review* (5 February 2013): 9-13. The article discusses the interagency problems and lack of synchronization of efforts toward achieving United States' strategic aims in Mali.

<u>Challenges to "Shock and Awe" Stability Operations</u>

Several books that comprehensively cover nation-building operations state there is a

"golden hour" directly following Phase III operations.[227] To create a stable environment during

this short three to six month time period, coalition forces must surge a force of specialized assets

to include troops, police, civil administrators, humanitarian workers, and judicial and penal

experts.[228] This golden hour is the reason why the United States' military must have a way, a

methodology, or force capable of rapidly transitioning from Phase III to Phase IV. This raises the

question then, how does the United States get trained forces to conduct shock and awe operations

during the first six months of Phase IV? How does America rapidly deploy this force if they are

not already mobilized? Can the United States put an ad-hoc organization together within a year, a

force that is capable of entering theater during Phase III operations prepare to begin Phase IV?

Will the stability force have some type of educational or professional background in the particular

system they are trying to establish in the host country? Can a force that is not under an enlistment

contract be expected to remain in immature security environments until progress can be made? In

addition, the agency or organization put together must have the capability and capacity to achieve

the U.S.'s Grand Strategy. The changes within the American government and military since

World War II only further complicate interagency and nation-building operations.

As a byproduct of the professional military force, the military switched from a conscript

army, having general officers with professional backgrounds outside the military, to a volunteer

professional force with career officers. This change cut down on the level of expertise and

experience senior leaders had outside the military system. Another major change to DOD came

---

[227]Dobbins, *The Beginner's Guide,* 15, 50.

[228] The surge force entails a whole of government or whole of nation approach. The exact details and make up of this force is outside the scope of this monograph. However, Thomas Barnett provides an outline for what he calls the "system administrators" force. Barnett, *Blueprint for Action*, 23-43.

with the Goldwater-Nichols Department of Defense Reorganization Act of 1986. This act required officers to obtain three years of joint service before promotion to general officer. Although this act improved the military's internal working environment, it did little to increase experience outside the military system. Of the 63 three and four-star general officers in the U.S. Army, today, none have served three years on joint assignments outside the DOD.[229] The question is that if there is a deliberate handover of the lead for operations between Phase III and Phase IV, then why does the military not have a requirement for joint positions outside of DOD? Although the DOS has a vast amount of expertise in systems outside the military, the internal culture does not lend itself to an adaptable culture capable of facilitating the transition from combat to stability.[230]

American policy makers may direct military intervention to support countries arising from their own conflict or humanitarian disaster. The USAID participates or takes the lead during these situations. Appendix F provides a framework for success for societies emerging from conflict. However, the agency often lacks the capability and/or capacity to conduct these missions worldwide. The agency often contracts or starts various programs within nations emerging from conflict, but often requires the military to oversee the implementation. Many of these projects are inadequately completed due to unqualified military personnel overseeing the projects.

---

[229]Although several general officers served as Political-Military Advisors in various countries, these assignments were only one-year tours. U.S. Department of the Army, "General Officers Management Office, Resume," https://www.gomo.army.mil/ext/portal/ResumeArchive. aspx (accessed 9 December 2012).

[230]Fukuyama, 87.

Further Considerations

Many theorists believe that nation building will be the type of operations that will occupy U.S. forces for the next 20 years.[231] In today's operational environment, there are relatively few nations with a significant conventional military force to challenge the United States directly. Future conflicts will likely be against non-state actors, such as terrorist and irregular forces, utilizing unconventional weapons and conducting sporadic attacks. Only by sharing of the responsibilities for security and strengthening multinational alliances will the global security and stability improve. Capacity building operations help developing and failing nations secure themselves, which in turn enhances American security and allows DOD to focus on fewer, strategic areas.

No longer is the DOD working in a seemingly unconstrained resource environment. Budget cuts will force DOD to relook its current force structure and methods to achieve its strategic objectives.[232] Cuts in force structure might further decrease the military's capability to rapidly, but effectively transition from Phase III to Phase IV. The United States must study varying governmental approaches to nation-building operations in order to properly structure any new holistic approach. According to the National Security Strategy joint, interagency, and international operations are required to secure U.S. interest and security under more constrained future conditions.

Closing

In order to effectively transition from Phase III dominated operations to Phase IV stability, the military must adapt aspects within the DOTMLPF framework to better recognize the

---

[231]John A Nagl, *Institutionalizing Adaptation.* Center for a New American Security, Online, http://www.cnas.org/node/130 (accessed 02 August 2012).

[232]Joint Force 2020, 4.

impacts that Phases 0 through Phase III have on the country's PMESII systems; establish a better understanding and working relationship with other governmental departments outside the military to rapidly facilitate transition; and adapt its means to increase the ways available to political decision makers to achieve their desired goals. The DOD must take a greater role in facilitating interagency, intergovernmental, and multinational cooperation in order to achieve the grand strategy outlined by the President.

The United States' new testament philosophy has shown that it prevents conflict and improves collective security, which is why the basic concepts remain as the foundation in its grand strategy. With stability comes improved economic development through trade, which can improve the quality of life in developing nations. The military must work with its inter-governmental partners and international allies to save resources and give legitimacy to any future operation. However, no organization or service within DOD is properly structure to synchronize the creation of globalized institutions as outlined in the National Security Strategy. Nation building, it appears, is the inescapable responsibility of the world's only superpower.[233] Nation building demands a holistic approach, conducted by professionals experienced within the system in order to be successful. The military must either develop the capability within themselves or develop the methodology to rapidly deploy a cohesive organization to win the peace after the war.

---

[233]Dobbins and Lal, *America's Role in Nation-Building*, xv.

APPENDIX A: NOTIONAL OPERATION PLAN PHASES VERSUS LEVEL OF MILITARY EFFORT

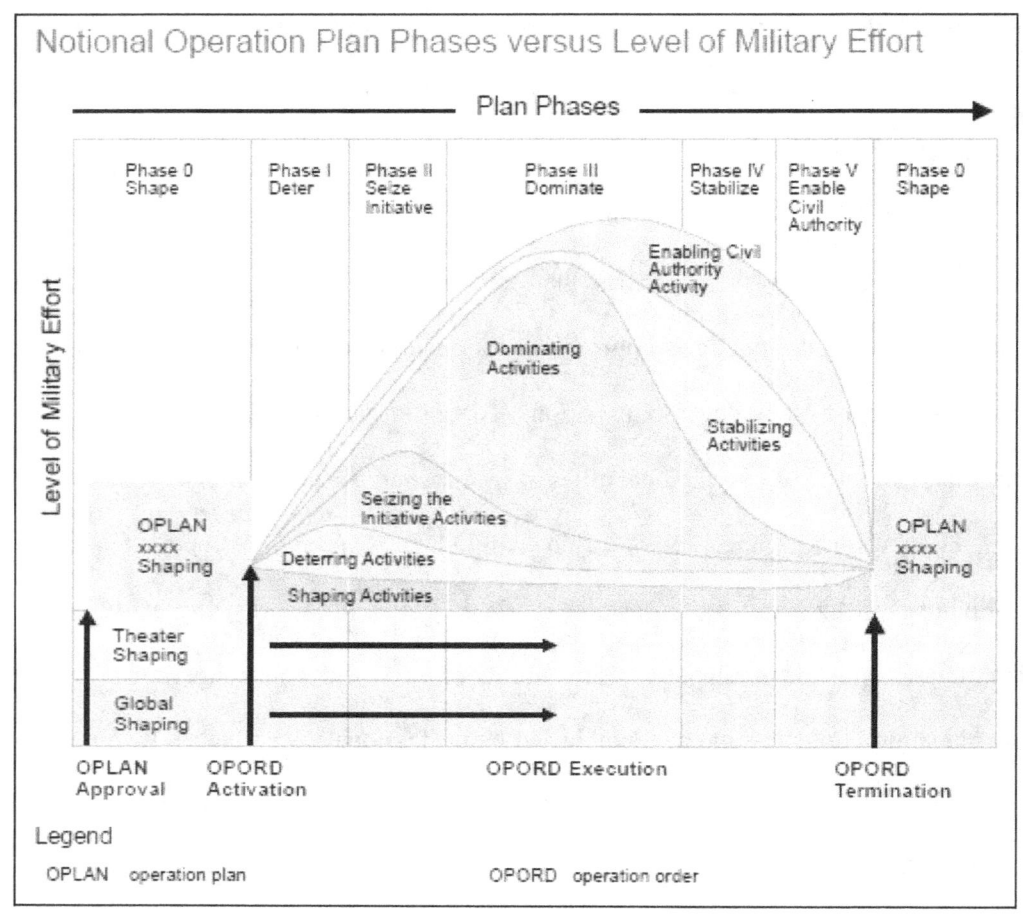

Source: *Department of Defense, Joint Publication 3-0, Joint Operations, (Washington: Headquarters, Department of Defense, 11 August 2011), V-6.*

APPENDIX B: NOTIONAL BALANCE OF OFFENSIVE, DEFENSIVE, AND STABILITY OPERATIONS

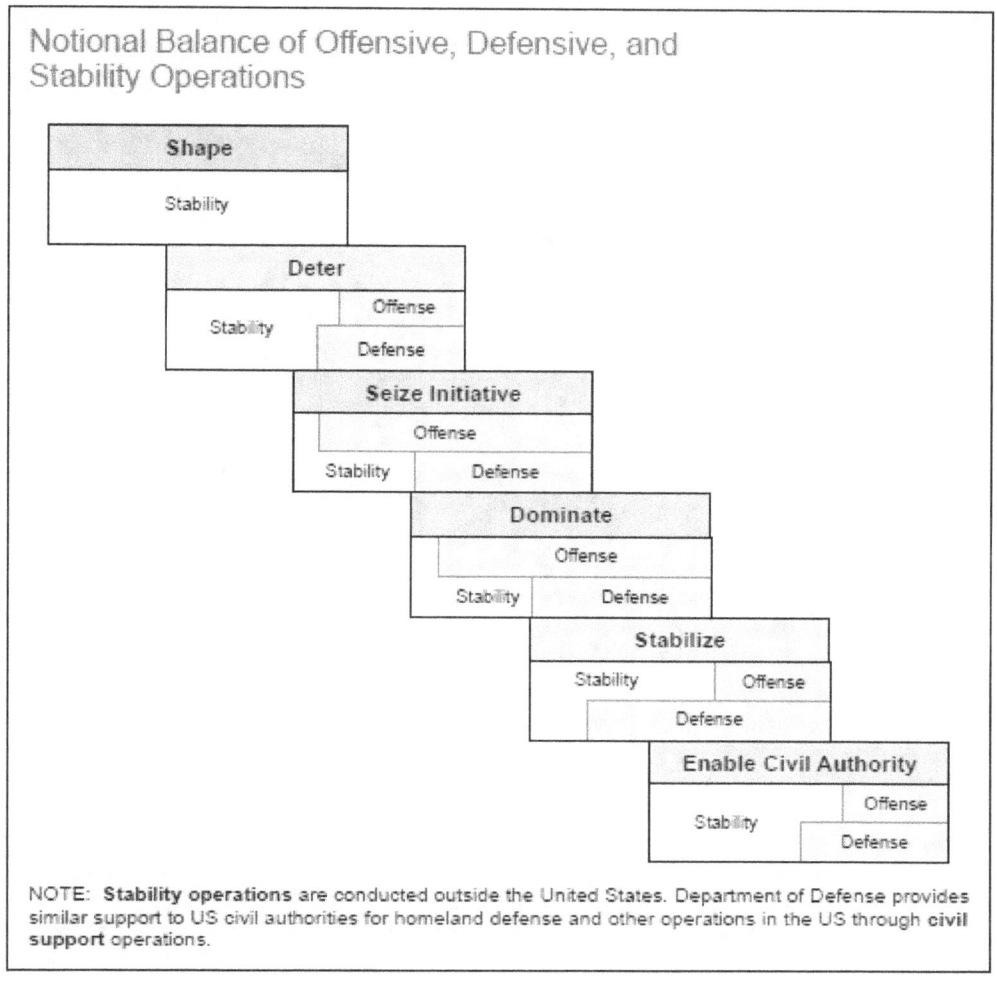

Source: Department of Defense, Joint Publication 3-0, Joint Operations, (Washington: Headquarters, Department of Defense, 11 August 2011), V-36.

Source: Training and Doctrine Command, TRADOC Pam 525-8-4, U.S. Army Concept for Building Partner Capacity, (Fort Eustis, VA: Headquarters, Department of the Army, 11 August 2011), 4.

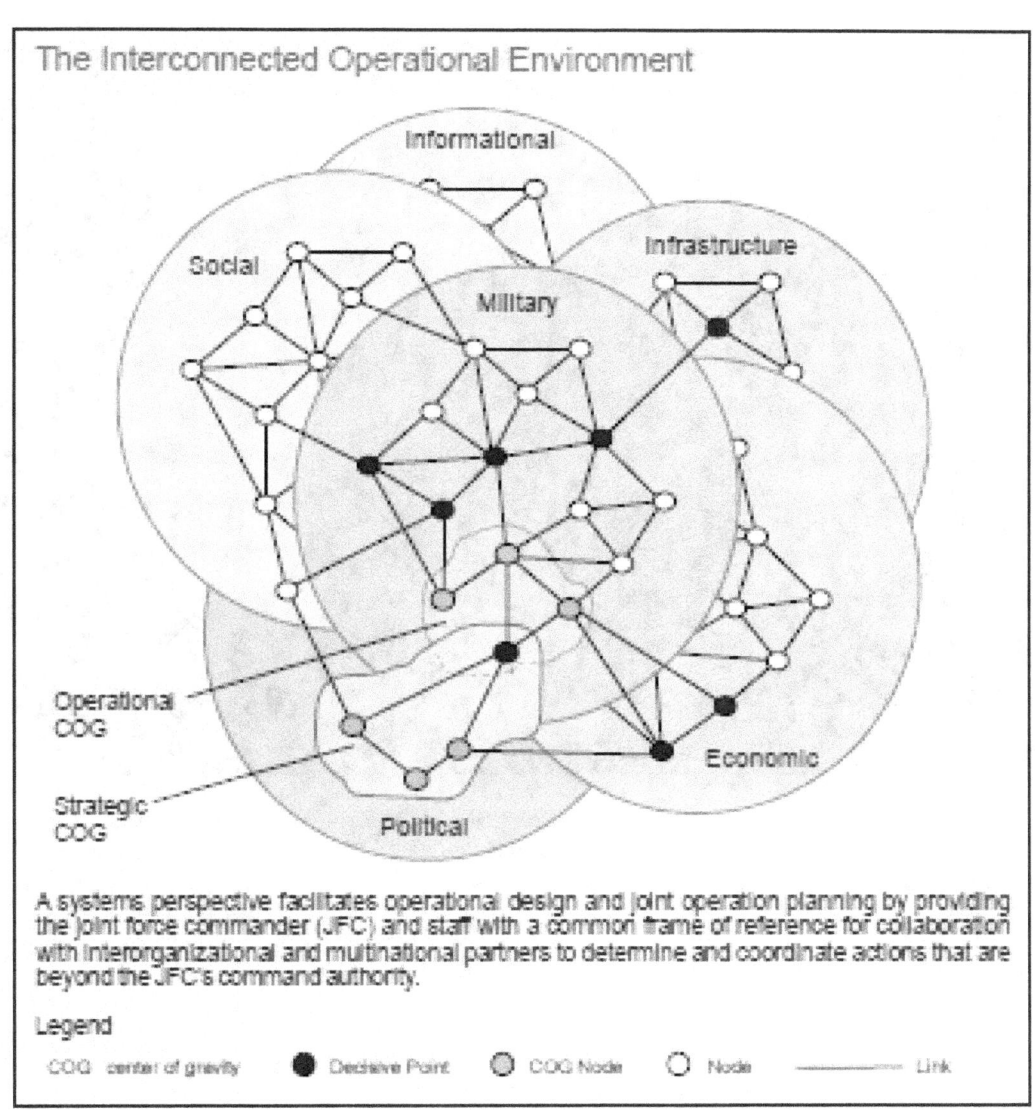

Source: Department of Defense, Joint Publication 3-0, Joint Operations, (Washington: Headquarters, Department of Defense, 11 August 2011), IV-5.

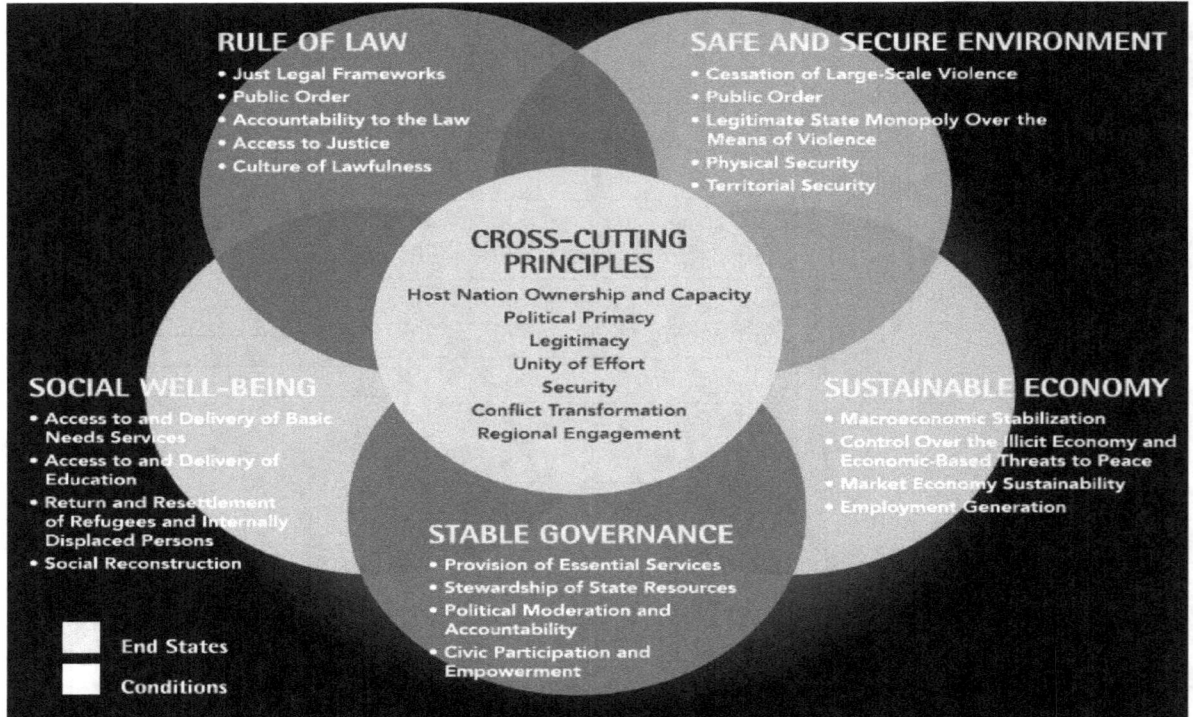

Source: U.S.Department of the Army Peacekeeping and Stability Operations Institute. Guiding Principles for Stabilization and Reconstruction, Washington, DC: United States Institute of Peace Press, 2009. 2-8.

BIBLIOGRAPHY

Books and Journals

Bacevich, Andrew J., *American Empire: The Realities and Consequences of U.S. Diplomacy.* Cambridge, MA/London, 2002.

Barnett, Thomas P.M. *The Pentagon's New Map: War and Peace in the Twenty-First Century.* New York: G.F. Putnam's Sons. 2004.

Barnett, Thomas P.M. *Blueprint for Action, A Future Worth Creating.* New York: Berkley Trade. 2006

Barnett, Thomas P.M. *Great Powers: America and the World After Bush.* New York: Berkley Trade. 2010

Bertalanffy, Ludwig von. *General System Theory.* (New York, 1968) 1st Edition, 1973, Penguin University Press Edition, 1975, 5th Edition.

Bielakowski, Alexander M. "Mechanization in the Interwar U.S. Cavalry." Excerpt from *U.S. Army Cavalry Officers and the Issue of Mechanization*, 1916-1940. PhD diss., Kansas State University, 2002.

Brewer, Susan A. *Why America Fights: Patriotism and War Propaganda from the Philippines to Iraq.* New York: Oxford University Press, USA, 2009.

Clausewitz, Carl von. *On War.* Edited and translated by Michael Howard and Peter Paret. Princeton. NJ: Princeton University Press, 1976.

DeBenedetti, Charles. *The Peace Reform in American History.* Bloomington, IN: 1980.

Diamond, Jared. *Guns, Germs and Steel.* 2nd ed. 5 vols, New York, New York: W.W. Norton and Company, Inc., 2001.

Dobbins, James. *After the War: Nation-Building from FDR to George W. Bush.* Santa Monica, CA: Rand Publishing, 2008.

Dobbins, James, and Rollie Lal. *America's Role in Nation-Building: from Germany to Iraq.* Santa Monica, CA: RAND Corporation, 2003.

Dobbins, James, Seth G. Jones, Keith Crane, and Beth Cole DeGrasse. *The Beginner's Guide to Nation-Building.* Santa Monica, CA: Rand Publishing, 2007.

Dolman, Everett Carl. *Pure Strategy: Power and Principle in the Space and Information Age.* New York, Frank Cass, 2005.

Dorner, Dietrich. *The Logic of Failure: Recognizing and Avoiding Error in Complex Situations.* Reading, MA.: Basic Books, 1997.

Douhet, Giulio. "Aerial Warfare." *The Command of the Air.* USAF Warrior Studies. Washington. DC: Office of Air Force History, 1983.

Friedman, Thomas L. *The Lexus and the Olive Tree*. New York: Farrar, Straus and Giroux, 2000.

Ferguson, Niall. *Colossus: The Rise and Fall of the American Empire*. New York: Penguin Books, 2005.

Fukuyama, Francis, ed. *Nation-Building: Beyond Afghanistan and Iraq*. Baltimore: The Johns Hopkins University Press, 2006.

George, Alexander L., and Andrew Bennett. *Case Studies and Theory Development in the Social Sciences*. Cambridge, MA: The MIT Press, 2005.

Gharajedaghi, Jamshid. *Systems Thinking: Managing Chaos and Complexity*, second edition. Elsevier: Butterworth-Heinemann, 2006.

Gordon, Michael R. "The Strategy to Secure Iraq Did Not Foresee a 2nd War." *New York Times*. 19 October 2004.

Gordon, Michael R., and Bernard E. Trainor. *Cobra II: the Inside Story of the Invasion and Occupation of Iraq*. New York: Pantheon, 2006.

Gray, Colin S. *War, Peace and International Relations: an Introduction to Strategic History*. London: Routledge, 2007.

Griffith, Robert K. Jr. *The U.S. Army's Transition to the All-Volunteer Force 1968-1974*. Center for Military History. United States Army, Washington, DC, 1997.

Hart, B.H. Liddell. *Strategy*. 2nd ed. New York, New York: Praeger Publishers, Inc., 1974.

Herring, George C. *From Colony to Superpower: U.S. Foreign Relations Since 1776*. New York: Oxford University Press, USA, 2008.

Huntington, Samuel P. *The Clash of Civilizations and the Remaking of World Order*. New York: Simon & Schuster, 1998.

Ikenberry, G. John. *After Victory: Institutions, Strategic Restraint, and the Rebuilding of Order After Major Wars*. Princeton: Princeton University Press, 2001.

Jervis, Robert. *System Effects*. Princeton, New Jersey: Princeton University Press, 1998.

Jomini, Baron de. *Summary of the Art of War*. Translated from the French by Capt. G. H. Mendell and Lieut W.P. Craighill, Westport, CT: Greenwood, 1992. First Published by J.B. Lippincott & Co.

Kalyvas, Stathis N. *The Logic of Violence in Civil War*. New York, NY: Cambridge University Press, 2006.

Linn, Brian McAllister. *The U.S. Army and Counterinsurgency in the Philippine War, 1899-1902*. Chapel Hill: University of North Carolina Press, 1989.

Mahnken, Thomas, and Joseph A. Maiolo, eds. *Strategic Studies: a Reader*. New York: Routledge, 2008.

Matheny, Michael R. *Carrying the War to the Enemy: American Operational Art to 1945.* Norman, Okla.: Univ of Oklahoma Pr (Trd), 2011.

McDougall, Walter. *Promised Land, Crusader State: the American Encounter with the World Since 1776.* Reprint ed. Boston: Mariner Books, 1998.

Mead, Walter R. *Special Providence: American Foreign Policy and How It Changed the World.* New York: Taylor & Francis Books, Inc., 2002.

Moltke, Helmuth von. *Moltke On the Art of War: Selected Writings.* New York: Presidio Press, 1995.

Naveh, Shimon. *In Pursuit of Military Excellence*: *The Evolution of Operational Theory.* Portland: Frank Cass, 1997.North, Douglass C. "Institutions," *Journal of Economic Perspectives.* Issue no. 1 (winter), 1991.

Nye Jr., Joseph S. *Soft Power: the Means to Success in World Politics.* New York: PublicAffairs, 2005.

Pape, Robert A. *Bombing to Win: Air Power and Coercion in War.* Ithaca, N.Y.: Cornell University Press, 1996.

Ricks, Thomas E. *Fiasco: the American Military Adventure in Iraq, 2003 to 2005.* Reprint ed. New York, NY: Penguin Books, 2007.

Sen, Amartya. *Development as Freedom.* New York: Anchor Books, 1999.

Senge, Peter M. *The Fifth Discipline: the Art and Practice of the Learning Organization.* Rev. and updated. ed. New York: Crown Business, 2006.

Tzu, Sun. *The Art of War.* New York, NY: Barnes & Noble Classics, 2003.

Warner, Lesley A. "Capacity Building Key to AFRICOM's Mission." *World Politics Review* (30 February 2013): 9-13.

Government Documents

Office of the President. *The National Security Strategy of the United States of America,* Washington, DC: The White House, January 1987.

Office of the President. *The National Security Strategy of the United States of America,* Washington, DC: The White House, May 2010.

Office of the President. *The National Security Strategy of the United States of America,* Washington, DC: The White House, September 2002.

U.S. Army TRADOC G2. TRADOC Intelligence Support Activity – Threats, *TRISA's Top 10 Potential Operational Environments.* Fort Leavenworth, KS. 30 January 2012.

U.S. Department of the Army. *Counterinsurgency Operations.* Field Manual 3-24, Washington, DC: Department of the Army, 2009.

U.S. Department of the Army. *Operations*. Army Doctrine Publication 3-0. Washington, DC: Department of the Army, 11 October 2011.

U.S. Department of the Army. *Operations*. Field Manual 3-0. Washington, DC: Department of the Army, 14 June 2001.

U.S. Department of the Army Peacekeeping and Stability Operations Institute. *Guiding Principles for Stabilization and Reconstruction*, Washington, DC: United States Institute of Peace Press, 2009. 2-8.

U.S. Department of the Army. *Stability Operations*. Field Manual 3-07, Washington, DC: Department of the Army, October 2008.

U.S. Department Of Defense. *Dictionary of Military and Associated Terms*. JP 1-02 Joint Dictionary and Terms, Washington DC: 08 November 2010.

U.S. Department Of Defense. *Joint Intelligence Preparation of the Operational Environment*. Joint Publication 2-01.3, Washington DC: 16 June 2009,

U.S. Department Of Defense. *Joint Operations*. Joint Publication 3-0. Washington DC: 11 August 2011.

U.S. Department Of Defense. *Joint Operation Planning*. Joint Publication 5-0. Washington DC: 11 August 2011.

U.S. Department Of Defense. *Stability Operations*. Joint Publication 3-07. Washington DC: 29 September 2011.

U.S. Department Of Defense. *Sustaining U.S. Global Leadership: Priorities for the 21st Century Defense*. Washington DC: January 2012.

U.S. Joint Chiefs of Staff. *Capstone Concept for Joint Operations: Joint Force 2020*. Washington DC: 10 September 2012.

U.S. Office of the Under Secretary of Defense for Policy. Deputy Assistant Secretary of Defense for Policy Planning. *Ungoverned Areas and Threats from Safe Havens*, by Robert D. Lamb. Open-file report, U.S. Geological Survey. Washington, DC, 2008.

Internet Sources

Avlon, John. "Romney on the Ropes." CNN Opinion. http://www.cnn.com/2012/10/23/opinion/ opinion-roundup-third-debate/index.html?iref=allsearch (accessed 21 November 2012).

Barnett, Thomas P.M. "National Security Strategy." Lecture. National Defense University. Fort McNair. Washington DC. 18 August 2006). http://www.c-spanvideo.org/program/ 193938-1 (accessed 3 December 2012).

Bush, George. "President Discusses Beginning of Operation Iraqi Freedom." The White House. http://georgewbush-whitehouse.archives.gov/news/releases/2003/03/20030322.html (accessed March 2013).

Confederation Congress. "An Ordinance for the Government of the Territory of the United States North West of the River Ohio." Library of Congress. http://www.loc.gov/rr/program/bib/ourdocs/northwest.html (accessed 8 December 2012).

Defense Security Cooperation Agency, "DSCA Historical Facts Book" http://www.dsca.mil/programs/biz-ops/factsbook/FiscalYearSeries-2010.pdf (accessed 8 December 2012).

Department of the Army. "WWII - European-African-Middle Eastern Theater." Center for Military History. http://www.history.army.mil/books/wwii/Occ-GY/ch12.htm (accessed 18 December 2012).

Gilewitch, Daniel. *Security Cooperation Strategic Guidance: Translating Strategy to Engagement.* DISAM Journal On-Line. http://www.disamjournal.org/articles/security-cooperation-strategic-and-operational-guidance-translating -strategy-to-engagement-773 (accessed 03 March 2013).

Gordon, Michael R. "Catastrophic Success: The Strategy to Secure Iraq Did Not Foresee a 2nd War." New York Times, 19 October 2004. http://www.nytimes.com/2004/10/19/international/19war.html?_r=0 (accessed 18 December 2012).

Joyner, James, "America and the World After Bush: Economics and Globalization," New Atlanticist. http://www.acus.org/new_atlanticist/america-and-world-after-bush-economics-and-globalization (accessed 3 December 2012).

Litan, Robert E. "The Road Ahead – How Do We Get There?" Entrepreneurship and Expeditionary Economics. http://www.kauffman.org/uploadedFiles/Enterpreneurship/International/expeditionary-economics-summit-panel-3.pdf (accessed 18 December 2012).

McDougall, Walter A. *The Constitutional History of U.S. Foreign Policy: 222 Years of Tension in the Twilight Zone.* (Philadelphia, PA: Foreign Policy Research Institute, September 2010). http://www.fpri.org/pubs/2010/McDougall.ConstitutionalHistoryUS Foreign Policy.pdf (accessed 10 November 2012).

Nagl, John A. *Institutionalizing Adaptation.* Center for a New American Security, Online http://www.cnas.org/node/130 (accessed 02 August 2012).

Office of the High Commissioner for Human Rights. "The Human Rights Impact of Economic Sanctions on Iraq." Campaign against Sanctions on Iraq. http://www.casi.org.uk/info/undocs/sanct31.pdf (accessed 29 November 2012).

Pei, Minxin. "Economic Institutions, Democracy, and Development." http://www.carnegieendowment.org/1999/02/26/economic-institutions-democracy-and-development/3i9 (accessed 18 December 2012).

Peterson, LTC Steven W. "Central but Inadequate: The Application of Theory in Operation Iraqi Freedom." http://www.dtic.mil/cgi-bin/GetTRDoc?AD=ada441663&Location=U2&doc=GetTRDoc.pdf (accessed 18 December 2012).

Powell, Colin. "Ideas and Consequences." Lecture, Aspen Ideas Festival, Aspen, Colorado, July 2007. http://www.theatlantic.com/magazine/archive/2007/10/ideas-and-consequences/306193/ (accessed 9 December 2012).

Stewart, Scott. "Mali Besieged by Fighters Fleeing Libya." STRATFOR Global Intelligence. http://www.stratfor.com/weekly/mali-besieged-fighters-fleeing-libya (accessed 27 November 2012).

Thucydides. "Melian Dialogue" available at: http://www.hks.harvard.edu/organizing/tools/Files/melians.pdf (accessed 2 December 2012).

United Nations. "United Nations Peacekeeping." United Nations. http://www.un.org/en/peacekeeping/ (accessed 7 November 2012).

U.S. Department of the Army. "General Officers Management Office, Resume," https://www.gomo.army.mil/ext/portal/ResumeArchive.aspx (accessed 9 December 2012).

U.S. Energy Information Administration. "Libya." http://www.eia.gov/cabs/libya/pdf.pdf (accessed 27 November 2012).

World Bank. "Iraq Country Brief." http://web.worldbank.org/WBSITE/EXTERNAL/COUNTRIES/MENAEXT/IRAQEXTN/0,menuPK:313115..pagePK:141132..piPK:141107..theSitePK:313105,00.html (accessed November 29, 2012).